D1013587

"Rosemary Flaaten lifts a curtain on the secretive ways in which we fail to display Christlike character in the workplace. I deeply appreciate how she grounds the entire book in the wisdom of Scripture and then applies those principles to real-life scenarios."

—Nancy Beach
Willow Creek Association
Author of *Gifted to Lead*

"Discover or rediscover your purpose at work. To be an agent of change who builds relational bridges one must read this book and execute its challenge."

—Paula A. Curtis
President & CEO, Opportunity International Canada

"Rosemary Flaaten has written an enlightening and truly Christian-based approach to professional relationships that arouses, inspires, provokes, and humbles the reader. Add this to your reading list if you're looking for a refreshing perspective on living your Christian values in your workplace."

—Helen Sunderland
Product Director, SAP Labs, California

"An exceptional book that eloquently captures the diverse range of challenges faced by Christian professional women in the workplace today."

—Rebecca Kung, bscm
Procurement Category Manager, International Oil and Gas Company

"After more than 40 years in a workplace, I gained insights from this thought-provoking read! Whether you're the boss or a new hire, you're sure to find help."

—Linda G. Hardin, DMin
General Coordinator, Women's Ministries, Church of the Nazarene

"Flaaten mixes her background in counseling, her passion for Scripture, and the collective experience of many women to create a book that is both practical and spiritual in its approach to building healthy relationships in the workplace."

—Georgia Shaffer
Pennsylvania Licensed Psychologist
Author of *Taking Out Your Emotional Trash*

"This material should be required reading for any woman entering the work world, since it will show you how to get along with anyone."

—Florence Littauer
Author of *Personality Plus* and *Silver Boxes*

A WOMAN and HER

Workplace

Building Healthy Relationships
from 9 to 5

Rosemary Flaaten

BEACON HILL PRESS
OF KANSAS CITY

Library of Congress Cataloging-in-Publication Data

Flaaten, Rosemary, 1965-
    A woman and her workplace : building healthy relationships from 9 to 5 / Rosemary Flaaten.
        p. cm.
    Includes bibliographical references.
    ISBN 978-0-8341-2523-0 (pbk.)
    1. Christian women—Religious life. 2. Work—religious aspects—Christianity. I. Title.
    BV4527.F594 2010
    248.8'43—dc22
                                                    2010023032

10 9 8 7 6 5 4 3 2 1

Contents

Acknowledgments

This book would not have become a reality if not for a multitude of women whose willingness to tell their stories became the impetus for the eventual outline. I thank each of you for sharing the good, the bad, and the ugly. I admire your courage and fortitude.

My thanks go to the eclectic group of readers who scoured the manuscript to offer insight and encouragement: Karin, Barbara, Daisy, Tim, Len, and Karen. Thank you also to the endorsers who gave your time to read and offer such strong support. I'm deeply grateful!

One woman believed in me when all I saw was my inadequacies and muddle and took time out of her full schedule to encourage and prod. Her experiences primed my creativity. Thank you, Irene Pfieffer!

Florence Littauer: One aptly spoken sentence in a brief conversation I had with you became the seed for this book. Your fervor for communicating truth was passed to me, and I caught it. I am your Timothy.

Norlee, my husband and the love of my life: You are my dearest friend, my greatest cheerleader, and my most rigorous editor. Twenty-five years is just the beginning!

I thank Beacon Hill Press of Kansas City, in particular Bonnie, Judi, Barry, and Jon. Your confidence in me and your support have truly been a blessing. You are an amazing team.

Without the inspiration infused by the Holy Spirit, this book would not have happened. I am humbled by God's calling on my life.

Introduction

Working women. It seems redundant to put the adjective *working* as a descriptor to women. All women work—and work hard. Eight-hour days would be a luxury. From before sunrise until long after sunset, women put their hands to the proverbial plow to get things done.

We may spend our days in a corner office with a view or our evenings cleaning corporate offices. Maybe we teach adults necessary life skills or nurse the elderly. Maybe we write computer programs or govern a municipal jurisdiction. Maybe we design bridges or spend the day welding the steel that holds those bridges together. Whether our jobs demand physical labor, mental acumen, creative ingenuity, or business astuteness, at one time or another we'll find ourselves struggling to build healthy relationships with those with whom we work.

We are ordinary women who get up every morning, dive into our responsibilities at home, then jump into our jobs. Sometimes we work because we enjoy what we do and feel personally fulfilled; at other times we endure it so we can put food on the table. Our families and our careers seem to coexist, but on different planes. We struggle to find and maintain a proper balance between our work lives and personal lives. We endeavor to live out our faith in a secular world—sometimes with the added challenge of a cranky boss or belligerent staff. Maybe we enjoy a few decent relationships at work, but overall those relationships could use some improvement. On some level we know that the health of our workplace relationships is affecting our ability to produce our best work.

Some of us are aware of our propensity to blame others for our iffy workplace relationships, but deep down we know that we must take responsibility for what lurks in our own hearts that impacts our ability to build healthy relationships. If we fail to deal with our own issues, strained relationships will follow us throughout our lives and will have an impact on realizing our God-given potential. It's our hearts that direct our actions and stimulate life. It's our hearts that are lacerated when hurtful words are spoken or quicken with pleasure when things are running smoothly. It's our hearts that love.

Difficult workplace relationships threaten to erode, crumble, or destroy the connections we have with our coworkers. Pride, deception, anger, judgmental attitudes, and envy have the potential to bring our careers to a halt, ruin our relationships, and strip us of our emotional and spiritual health. Thus we must be prepared to counteract these relationships by bringing biblical corrective measures into the mix. By fostering humility, pride will be vanquished, integrity will take the place of deceit, and forgiveness will overcome anger. Extending grace will dissolve judgment, and living a life of celebration will end envy. Allowing God to enact His great reversal in our hearts will enable us to build healthy relationships in the work environment.

Many books have been written to examine the relationships of daughters, mothers, wives, sisters, and friends. But there's a vacuum when it comes to workplace relationships, particularly from the perspective of what's happening in the hearts of women as they work and interact with others. Applying God's truths to change our hearts will synergize our relationships with Him and our coworkers.

My hope is that this book will draw you into a deeper and more intimate relationship with Jesus. A changed heart that puts God first and then seeks to love others will have a profoundly positive effect on your workplace.

1 Building the Relationship Bridge

I felt all alone despite being surrounded by people. I knew no one, and no one knew me. I was sitting in a room with thirty other staff members. Some were new hires like me, some had enough years of experience to feel comfortable, and others were close to retirement. I felt a mix of exhilaration and fear as I started my first real full-time job following college.

I was entering the realm of workplace relationships.

That first day on the job not only did I feel unprepared to teach my inaugural class of third-grade students, but I also was keenly aware that I was going to need adult relational skills beyond what I had needed up to that point. There would be a whole new set of colleagues in my life. That initial work experience taught me the tremendous effect workplace relationships would have on my ability to do my job, not to mention their effect on my emotional, physical, and spiritual wellbeing.

11

I assumed that many of my new coworkers would be nice, but I really had no idea if any of them would like me or if I would enjoy being in their company. Some appeared to be friendly immediately. Others seemed to carry chips on their shoulders. I feared that some of them would make working as a team quite challenging.

I had thought making the curriculum come alive for elementary school children would be the hard part, but I began to suspect that working with the people in that room was going to be harder still. I was full of enthusiasm and naivety, though, so I jumped into my job and started forming new relationships.

During my six-year tenure at that school, I developed many strong relationships. Some coworkers became friends with whom I enjoyed after-work activities. I often had lunch with some of my coworkers, sharing bits of our lives with each other, but these relationships never extended beyond the walls of the workplace. Others were cool and congenial and simply putting in the time and effort to accomplish the work. I remember spending most of an evening rehashing an argument I had had with a coworker, trying to understand her point of view and what I should have said differently, fearing the next day's interaction. I shudder now as I look back at my weak relational skills during those first years in the workplace.

Throughout my subsequent positions over the years I have learned so much about working with people. It would certainly be wonderful to work in a healthy environment where issues were dealt with quickly and fairly. However, the reality is that our workplace relationships are often less than ideal. You may work in an environment in which you report to a boss who's difficult to respect. You may work with staffmembers who give a great effort this week only to conspire mutiny the next. Some of us work alongside peers who have such different personalities from what we're used to that it not only hampers our productivity but often drives us crazy. Our relationships with male coworkers may present their own set of challenges for our emotional wellbeing. The women we work with range from our best friends to our greatest foes.

The people we connect with at work have a tremendous impact on our job satisfaction, our ability to deliver results, and our overall emotional, physical, and spiritual well-being. I've written this book to address a very real need: how can we build relationships in the workplace that are healthy and God-pleasing?

A Civil Engineer

I'm about as far as you can get from a scientific, analytical, engineer-type. I do okay balancing my checkbook, but talk to me about aerodynamics or metaphysics, and my eyes glaze over. Let me propose that in the workplace you take on the role of a "civil engineer."

The word "civil" refers to the citizens or individuals who belong to a society. When two individuals are in a relationship working for the same company or department, they belong to the same "society." Civil engineering is the discipline of designing, constructing, and maintaining both naturally and physically built environments, such as bridges. Metaphorically, our mandate as civil engineers is to design, build, and maintain relational bridges with coworkers.

The presenting problem is that we find ourselves on the opposite side of a relational chasm from the people with whom we work. In order to have a relationship, there needs to be a bridge that spans this relational expanse. Just as a civil engineer considers the environment and the application that a bridge will serve, likewise we must consider the person and the environment of the relationship as we choose the best method to construct a relational bridge.

Some bridges will develop naturally; others will take more time and effort. Some bridges can collapse, yet others withstand the torrents and relational quakes that strike over time. No two bridges are the same. Factors such as distance between shorelines, stability of the ground, and purpose of the bridge all affect their design. So it is in workplace relationships. We have associations that occur between a boss and staff, and we have peer interactions with both men and women. Some develop into lifelong friendships, while others stay superficial and aloof. At the very least we need to be congenial and professional in our relationships. Whatever the situation, a relationship requires a bridge to span the chasm that exists between us and the other person.

Start with the Foundation

When we begin a new job, we're faced with the daunting task of building relational bridges from the foundation up. Since no previous connections exist, we have the chance to start relationships afresh. We find ourselves wondering, *How will I ever get along with this person? How can I learn to relate to the people on this team so that I do my job to the best of my ability? My boss is a real mystery. How will I fill the demands that are placed on me?* As intimidating as it may seem to enter a workplace where everyone represents new relationships, the approach we take has the potential to prevent unhealthy relational patterns from forming.

When we've already been working with people for a period of time and the connection between us is not good, extra work will be needed to undo destructive relationship patterns. Identifying what is eroding the relationship is imperative to addressing the issues. Furthermore, we will need to make decisions as to what elements should be added to strengthen the connection.

Regardless of the kind of bridge that needs to be built—whether we're starting from scratch or doing repair work—the place to start is the foundation. There are many resources on best business practices and theories of building strong teams. There are also authors who write from a psychological perspective to help us understand the people around us. While recognizing that these practices, theories, and perspectives have their places in relationship building, I do not use them as the material for laying a strong foundation. The relational foundation must be rooted in a relationship with God. I believe that Jesus' teachings on relationships can change the way we connect and will result in healthy workplace relationships.

At the risk of being dismissed by those who would say that this approach has nothing to offer and that it's another mindless example of "the right answer is always Jesus," I challenge you to open your heart to the biblical truths presented in these pages. These ideas surely didn't originate with me. They come out of the holy words of Scripture. When we put God in His rightful first place, ideology that follows biblical teaching will be affirmed.

If we were to epitomize God into one characteristic and the effect of His presence in our lives, it would come down to this: *love*. When Jesus was asked which of the commandments was most important, He reduced the list to "'Love the Lord your God with all your heart and with all your soul and with all your mind.' This is the first and greatest commandment. And the second is like it: 'Love your neighbor as yourself'" (Matthew 22:37-39).

Later in the New Testament, Paul makes this statement: "Now these three remain: faith, hope and love. But the greatest of these is love" (1 Corinthians 13:13). The apostle John pinpoints it by saying, "God is love" (1 John 4:16). So when He pours himself into our receptive hearts, He pours in love. Think of this as the highest quality of cement that can be poured into pilings to create the firmest of foundations. God is never miserly with the amount of love He bestows on us. Our hearts can be overflowing with His love, and it's out of that spillage that we'll be full of love to pass on to our coworkers.

You may resist the idea of loving your coworkers when you can barely tolerate some of them. We love our parents, spouse, children, and best friends—but not all of our coworkers. The problem with this myopic view of giving love to only our closest relationships is the fact that Scripture commands us to pass on the love we have been given. Jesus went so far as to tell us to love our *enemies*. In the workplace that would include the terrible boss, the smelly or obnoxious man, the gossiping woman, the lazy new hire, and the ornery caretaker. How can we love chocolate or a new silk blouse but not the people God made in His own image? What can this God-love look like in the workplace?

I could fill many pages trying to describe love, but my attempts would be meager. So let's use 1 Corinthians 13 (*The Message*) to describe love in real life:

- Love is patient.
- Love is kind.
- It does not envy.
- It does not boast.
- It is not proud.
- It is not rude.
- It is not self-seeking.
- It is not easily angered.
- It keeps no record of wrongs.
- Love does not delight in evil but rejoices with the truth.
- It always protects.
- Love always trusts.
- Love always hopes.
- Love always perseveres.

Here is the same list revised to apply to the workplace—the day-to-day reality of cubicles, company cafeterias, staff meetings, and business trips:

- Because I love the people I work with, I will never give up on them.
- I will care more for others at my workplace than for myself.
- Because I choose to love my coworkers, I will not want what they have.
- Because I care about my coworkers, I will not strut or brag about my successes.
- Because I care about my coworkers, I will not force myself or my ideas on others.
- Because I care about my coworkers, I will not insist that it is "me first."
- Because I care about my coworkers, I won't fly off the handle.
- Because I care about my coworkers, I will forgive them and not keep score of their wrongs against me.
- As a way of showing that I care, I will not revel when others grovel.
- As a way of showing that I care, I will take pleasure only in the truth.
- Even when it is really difficult, I will choose to put up with as much as is possible without compromising the workplace values or my responsibility.
- I recognize that care grows as I trust God.
- I choose to be careful with criticism by reserving it for constructive feedback, and I will show care by always looking for the best in others.
- Because I care, I will not allow myself to dwell on the past.
- With God's help, I will not stop showing care for my coworkers.

I've interchanged the words *love* and *care* for a reason. In the workplace it's seldom appropriate to express your love for your coworkers. For example, if we were to go above and beyond our prescribed workload to help out a coworker with a task, and he or she were to ask why we had done so, it would probably not be fitting to say, "Because I love you." But we could certainly let the person know that we saw how big the task was and that we were concerned that it was affecting his or her emotional and physical health. Because we wanted our coworker to succeed at the task to continue to be healthy, we chose to help him or her.

We don't need to advertise that we love the people we work with or even that we're trying to love them. Simply keeping our hearts open to God so that His love continues to fill our hearts, the overflow will give us the love we need to care for those around us. Our ability to care starts with a heart attitude and evidences itself in actions.

Create a Pier of Trust

Once we have the foundational relationship with God and are dependent on being filled with His love to pass on to others, we're now ready to build a pier in the middle of the chasm. This pier is trust, and trust rests on the foundation of a relationship with God and the love it produces. It's essential to all relationships, not only workplace relationships. Whether our relationship realities are with supervisors, staff, or peers, when we work with others we're working as part of a team.

This quote from Patrick Lencioni's *The Five Dysfunctions of a Team* refers specifically to teams, which are the groups of people with whom we work:

> Trust lies at the heart of a functioning, cohesive team. Trust is the confidence among team members that their peers' intentions are good and that there is no reason to be protective or careful around the group. In essence, teammates must get comfortable being vulnerable with one another.[1]

Lencioni goes on to say,

It is only when team members are truly comfortable being exposed to one another that they begin to act without concern for protecting themselves. As a result, they can focus their energy and attention completely on the job at hand, rather than on being strategically disingenuous or political with one another.[2]

He then gives a list of the attributes exhibited by members of trusting teams that has great similarity to the list of loving attributes from 1 Corinthians 13 that we just examined.

- Admit weakness and mistakes.
- Ask for help.
- Accept questions and input about their areas of responsibility.
- Give one another the benefit of the doubt before arriving at a negative conclusion.
- Take risks in offering feedback and assistance.
- Appreciate and tap into one another's skills and experiences.
- Focus time and energy on important issues, not politics.
- Offer and accept apologies without hesitation.
- Look forward to meetings and other opportunities to work as a group.[3]

Pouring love and care into our workplace relationships will create an environment where trust is built. Trust is the center pier that rests on our foundation of God and is the bridge that crosses the relational chasm. If we have not created an environment of trust, the relational bridge will collapse.

Erosive Factors

Unfortunately, we don't live in a perfect world. If we did, our interactions with others would always be healthy. There would be nothing threatening to undermine, break down, or destroy the relational bridge.

When designing a bridge, an engineer must consider the factors that will erode its foundation, placing a strain on the bridge. Relationally, there will be similar threatening dynamics at play, depending on whether we're interacting with the boss, employees, or male or female coworkers. Engineers are good at performing something called "root cause analysis." Where the general public sees a collapsed bridge and speculates whether the collapse was due to an overloaded truck or a careless design engineer, a knowledgeable engineer may be able to trace the collapse to the corrosion of many small rivets caused by not following the prescribed maintenance program.

I remember watching with horror the collapse of an interstate bridge spanning the Mississippi River in Minneapolis in 2007. It seemed inconceivable that a bridge could appear to be sturdy and fully functional and then crumble without warning, causing mayhem, destruction, and death. I also recall the powerful earthquake that shook the San Francisco Bay area in 1989, causing freeways and overpasses to collapse.

In both cases, on-location television reporters made profound statements about the magnitude of the mess that was unfolding and posed questions about how something so destructive could possibly have been avoided.

The same profound observation could also relate to our relationships. *Why are we so messed up? How did we get into such a relational mess?* One moment everything is seemingly fine; then suddenly the relational bridge starts to collapse. It may have been caused by something with the magnitude of an earthquake that shakes and even destroys the relationship. Conversely, it can be a small and seemingly insignificant chain that brings about the erosion and collapse.

In order to answer the question of why we're so messed up, we need to reenact the collapse of relationships at the beginning of time in the Garden of Eden. At creation God designed things to be in harmony. Adam and Eve had the perfect relationship, and they lived in harmony with God, each other, and nature. In this perfect environment God walked with them and poured His goodness and peace into them. It was paradise.

Then the fall occurred, and sin entered the equation. Instead of being open and receptive to allow the free flow between God and themselves, Adam and Eve became ashamed and withdrawn. Instead of being God- and other-focused, they became self-focused. Instead of being sinless and in perfect harmony with God, pride, deception, anger, judgment, and envy entered their relationships.

The fall created a significant shift in human interaction. This shift has caused a permanent fracture in our relationships that has caused the integrity of our relational bridges to be at risk.

The root cause analysis of our relational issues does not point to our work environment, our childhood deficiencies, or even the obnoxious people who work next to us. The root cause of relational issues is sin. We need first to ask God to search our own hearts to see if there's any wicked way in us and to show us the effect it has on our relationships. This is not easy, as our tendency is to see the issue as being the result of wicked ways in *others*.

Our own sin may not be the only contributor to the problem, because others also bring their sinfulness to the relational equation. This makes it very easy to collect evidence against and place the blame on someone else. It's also more comfortable to focus on others' faults than it is to focus on the good that God is working within them. However, until we can see more of the goodness of God within them than the sin within them, we'll have little desire to build a bridge to them. In effect, we place too little value upon them.

As we read Scripture and see the value that Christ placed on thieves, prostitutes, and liars, how can we, who are not God, place a lesser value on our coworkers than He? We need to pray the same prayer that King David penned: "Investigate my life, O God, find out everything about me; Cross-examine and test me, get a clear picture of what I'm about; See for yourself whether I've done anything wrong—then guide me on the road to eternal life" (Psalm 139:23-24, TM).

Toxic relational issues, caused by our sin as well as the sin of others, permeate our workplace and threaten to erode our relational bridges. They're pervasive and real and can ruin our relationships, strip us of our emotional and spiritual health, and bring our careers to a halt. We must be prepared with a strategy that counters the effects of these relational issues. Just as our attempts to create a humanly contrived love will be deficient, so our attempts to fix our relationships will be meager at best. "God didn't go to all the trouble of sending his Son merely to point an accusing finger, telling the world how bad it was. He came to help, to put the world right again" (John 3:17, TM). That is a relational remedy—putting the world right again to counter the effects of sin.

Corrective Measures

Identifying the root problem and being offered a solution does not mean that healthy relational bridges are constructed. Simply considering a solution to the problem isn't enough; it must be acted upon. "Faith by itself, if not accompanied by action, is dead" (James 2:17). An engineer knows that adding steel to a bridge can enhance its strength. How ludicrous it would be simply to add the steel as a decorative feature rather than as a means of improving its load-bearing capacity!

The absurdness of this decision is similar to what Christ spoke of at the end of his Sermon on the Mount. Here are His paraphrased words:

Why are you so polite with me, always saying "Yes, sir," and "That's right, sir," but never doing a thing I tell you? These words I speak to you are not mere additions to your life, homeowner improvements to your standard of living. They are foundation words, words to build a life on. If you work the words into your life, you are like a smart carpenter who dug deep and laid the foundation of his house on bedrock. When the river burst its banks and crashed against the house, nothing could shake it; it was built to last. But if you just use my words in Bible studies and don't work them into your life, you are like a dumb carpenter who built a house but skipped the foundation. When the swollen river came crashing in, it collapsed like a house of cards. It was a total loss (*Luke 6:46-49, TM*).

God's truth, when worked into our hearts, gives us the corrective measures to counteract sin. If we act upon the corrective measures He offers, we'll experience relational change. "Don't fool yourself into thinking that you are listening when you are anything but, letting the Word go in one ear and out the other. Act on what you hear!" (James 1:22, TM).

The Bridge That Jesus Built

God's love is boundless, measureless, and fathomless. People who have never experienced the love of God are thirsty for it. We have it within us, not because of anything we have done to deserve it but simply because while we were yet sinners, Christ showed his great love for us by dying for the forgiveness of our sins (Romans 5:8). The chasm between a holy God and us, which was created by our sin, can be bridged only by Jesus. The design of this relational bridge is in the shape of a cross. God does not desire that anyone would end this life on earth without having a relationship with Him. It is His intent that every person would choose to bridge the chasm by accepting the sacrifice of Jesus on the Cross. If you're reading this and know that the chasm between you and God remains, ask for His forgiveness, and accept the gift of love He offers. It's that simple. Confess. Accept. Believe.

You'll hear a lot about Esther, who lived more than twenty-one centuries ago, in this book. You'll also hear from many twenty-first-century women who are our counterparts today. Though Esther and women of today are of two different times and two different cultures, the synergy in their stories is remarkable. Esther took on the challenges of life, as you and I do; Esther knew the sting of hardship and heartache, as you and I do; Esther knew what it was like to face fear and to make risky decisions that required more of her than she knew she had, as you and I do.

You and I and Esther have all found ourselves in roles and situations we never expected. We represent thousands—even millions—of women down through the ages who have taken on relational workplace challenges that threatened to undo them. Instead of allowing life to defeat us, though, we accept the challenge to courageously rise and make a difference.

The Story of Esther

Many of the biblical examples I have chosen come from the story of Esther. She was a culturally displaced orphan who became a queen, living more than twenty-one centuries ago. You may protest that Esther has nothing of value to say to women who have put in a great deal of hard work to accomplish the real jobs we go to each day. Our reality opposes this beauty queen. One woman responded to the notion of looking at Esther as a role model by candidly querying, "Can you tell me why you think Esther is a model for women in the workplace today? I can see her having something to say to contestants on 'The Bachelor,' and I admire Esther's courage, but the rest seems like a stretch between cultures. How many times are we called to hang our enemies, sleep with the boss, or start a massacre?"

I would encourage you to read the story of Esther with an open mind and heart to discover how she handled the dilemmas of her life and the impact her decisions had on her relationships. Esther's workplace included a foster home, a palace, a royal bedroom, and a divided nation. However, her job as queen of Persia need not be any more significant in the course of history than your present work situation.

Modern-day Esthers

Alongside Esther are you and me. We represent millions of women down through the ages who have taken on the challenge of developing strong relationships and through this have impacted our worlds. We will spend time discovering, learning from, and celebrating our stories. These stories could be your story.

I have had a variety of working relationships throughout my life. I've worked with farm laborers; cared for the elderly and disabled beside cleaning and nursing staff; taught alongside teachers in Canada, Haiti, and Africa; ministered next to pastoral staff in small and mega churches; and have partnered with a variety of professional speakers, marketers, and publications staff. Apart from writing and speaking, I presently volunteer with a ministry—Professional Women's Network—that encourages women who work within the corporate environment to deepen their relationships with God and others. Some of my roles have been quite monotonous and other times technically demanding. The element that kept these jobs interesting, successful, and enduring was relationships.

I would love to be able to report that every workplace relationship I've been involved in has been strong and life-giving. But I, like you, have struggled to make these relationships healthy. As I recall the many and varied people I have worked with, I hold a mixture of joy and regret. However, hope comes in allowing God to work change in my heart that transforms me to be more like Him. Then, as I act upon the opportunities He presents to build relational bridges, connections with people develop where previously there was an unapproachable chasm. This creates the opportunity for a positive relational legacy.

Many times I've foolishly thought the impact was only on my life, but in retrospect I can see that God placed me in those positions "for such a time as this" (Esther 4:14). We've all been given skills and abilities to equip us to fulfill our calling to accomplish a task and to build relational bridges. As our relationships with God become more intimate, we'll be spurred on to see our relationships with others deepen, thus prompting them to open up to God (Matthew 5:16, TM). Deeper relationship with God and with others is our ultimate calling.

In the chapters that follow, we'll investigate five sins—pride, deception, anger, judgment, and envy—and the devastating effects they have on relationships. Each of these patterns of relating, which were inherited from Adam and Eve, will erode the foundation of God's plan. If left unchecked, they can even destroy relationships.

But there's hope. Scripture offers corrective measures that, if applied to our relationships, will build and maintain healthy relationships.

Verses to Study

Matthew 22:37-39

1 Corinthians 13:13

James 1:22

1 John 4:16

Romans 5:8

John 3:17

Esther 4:4

James 17-26

Matthew 5:16

Questions for Reflection

1. Identify people from your past or present workplace or place of volunteering or community with whom you've had a difficult relationship. Attempt to make a list that identifies the issues that they brought to the relationship and the issues you contributed. Remember that issues will come from both sides.

2. Identify what part of showing loving care to your coworkers is difficult. Where do you feel a resistance to this principle?

3. What do you do in your workplace relationships that prompts others to open up to you?

2 Pride Vanquished by Humility

The room was abuzz. Everybody who was anybody had been invited. I was feeling pretty good that my accomplishments and connections had afforded me a seat at this event. I had bought a new suit to make sure I would fit in. To tell the truth, I was hoping my new suit would help me stand out just a notch above the rest.

With my shoulders squared, chin held high, and a slight swagger to my step, I crossed the room to the hors d'oeuvres. As I neared that side of the room, I caught the eye of a colleague—someone I was hoping to impress. After stopping briefly to load up on an array of delicacies, I swung around to head in her direction. My bubble of self-obsession did not afford me the wherewithal to be cognizant of anyone around me who might also be focused on getting somewhere else. Let's just say that my food connected with her food, and the result was humiliation on a platter.

I drew everyone's attention all right, but it was not because of my poise, outfit, abilities, or credentials. I had tripped on my pride. Spinach balls, seafood sauce, and a touch of chocolate now decorated my new suit. My sense of superiority nosedived, and I realized that indeed, pride had come before a fall.

Pride. Arrogance. Cockiness. Egotism. The list leaves us with an unpleasant aftertaste, yet if we're really honest, we all carry around some degree of vanity. Psychologists would affirm that we require a certain amount of pride and sense of self-worth to take on the challenges of life. I agree, but I've also found that there's a very fine line between a healthy self-esteem and an inflated sense of importance.

The attempts we make to inflate our abilities, importance, and worth are rooted in the fear that we don't have what it takes. If we look back to the Garden of Eden, the serpent planted seeds of doubt in the minds of Adam and Eve as to whether or not God could be trusted. He hinted that they would be better off if they took matters into their own hands (see Genesis 3:1-5). Those seeds of doubt took root, and what developed in humanity was *pride.* Pride keeps us from admitting our need for and continued dependence upon God.

Consciously and subconsciously, we look for ways to confirm that there must be some way to make life work without God. When things go well, it reaffirms our independence and the assumption that we really don't need Him. When things go downhill, we believe the lie that maybe life would be better if we didn't have to attempt to appease God. Whichever way we turn, pride seems to be there waiting to trip us up, woo us into independence, or eat away at our God-given sense of worth. Psalm 10:4 says, "In his pride the wicked does not seek him; in all his thoughts there is no room for God." The paraphrase of this passage in *The Message* states, "The wicked snub God, their noses stuck high in the air. Their graffiti are scrawled on the walls: 'Catch us if you can!' 'God is dead.'"

The same way that love poured into our hearts from God spills out as care for the people around us, so pride that separates us from God will have devastating effects on our horizontal relationships.

Erin's Story

Erin had worked hard at her position at a prestigious law firm. She had risen through the ranks, mainly because she was known for her diligence and keen attention to detail. She had recently received a promotion that involved the responsibility of implementing twenty different projects, a task previously undertaken by her boss.

With elevated confidence and a coy sense of independence, Erin set out to accomplish these tasks. The first nineteen were executed flawlessly. Their success seemed to shine even more brightly because only her name had been attached to them. She would get full kudos for the success. Self-congratulatory thoughts flitted through her mind. *Look at me! Don't I look good? Who needs the boss when he's got such a competent assistant?*

Riding high, she set about executing the last project. She had this nagging sense that something was supposed to be done differently with this one, but she sloughed it off based on the success of the previous ones. She knew what she was doing. Let's get this project over and done with. She imagined the next project given to her would be even more grandiose.

It had not been her intent to take the credit for this one, but her arrogant attitude had put her on a slippery slope. Erin's inflated sense of competency had steered her away from taking care of details that would have clarified the necessary protocol of including her boss's name on the last project. Within two minutes of the project being dispersed, Erin's boss was getting nasty communications from a sampling of over one hundred employees who noted the error made by Erin. Pride had led to her fall.

In her heart, she knew that it was her inflated sense of importance that had caused her to dismiss seeking counsel on these decisions. Independence established her own little kingdom. It was this same root of pride that resisted the notion of going to her boss with an apology. Nurturing this pride strengthened its hold on her heart.

Over the next couple of days, Erin was very busy with damage control. She and her boss did what they could, but the ripple effect was felt in numerous relationships throughout the firm. The greatest damage, though, had occurred in Erin's relationship with her boss. She knew she had a choice to make. She could remain stoic, attempting to make excuses for her mistake, or she could be real about her mistake that was rooted in pride, thus bringing humility to the situation. Remaining stoic had the potential to help her save face in the present. Humility seemed too close to humiliation. Erin struggled with the choice.

The Story of Esther

Haman may have been second in command in the Persian Empire, but he held the prize for being the number-one big shot in his own eyes. We don't know how or why Haman had been elevated to such a position of authority in the empire, but he likely would have needed to be a shrewd negotiator, a critical thinker, and a skilled militant. He had ready access to the king, and it's evident that the king thoroughly trusted not only his word but his judgment and abilities. With this kind of position under his belt, Haman had good reason to be proud.

When Mordecai would not bow down to Haman, it did not simply irritate Haman—it infuriated him. *Who does this Jew think he is? I am the mighty Haman.* I've taken some poetic freedom in that statement, because I want you to realize how deep the root of pride went in Haman's life. To understand where this prejudice came from, take a little trip back in history, back to the time when Israel's King Saul ruled.

At the height of his glory, Saul was told to destroy the long-time enemy of God's people, the Amalekites (1 Samuel 15:3). Rather than following this directive, Saul spared the life of King Agag, who was the ancestor of Haman. Saul's disobedience and rebellion, rooted in the feeling that he knew better than God what should be done, allowed the Amalekite people to remain and to come back hundreds of years later to again be a nemesis to the Jewish people. Saul's pride left the door open for the intense hatred and pride that infiltrated Haman's life. The root of pride does not die easily.

At some point though, the proud do fall (Daniel 4:37), and this is what happened to Haman. He embarked on a course to destroy his archrivals. His scheme to annihilate the Jews seemed flawless. All the pieces were falling into place, and to further feed his ego, his stature with the king and queen appeared to be increasing. On his way to stardom, the applause of those around him boosted his self-worth.

But God had plans that did not include the destruction of His people. In God's economy the proud do fall. "When pride comes, then comes disgrace" (Proverbs 11:2). Haman started the day by being full of his accomplishments, his importance to the empire, and assuming that the king wanted to esteem and honor him above all others. Within a few short hours he was groveling and pleading for his life before the Jewish queen. His final demise finds him hanging on the gallows he had built for Mordecai. Oh, how quickly the proud tumble!

Do You See the Issue?

Much as white crosses lining the ditch on a treacherous curve give evidence of those who did not heed the warning to slow down,

Scripture is full of warnings of the consequences of pride. Unfortunately, our sinful nature keeps us from admitting our pride. If we're sincere Christians, we know we should not entertain pride. Even pride in our ability not to be proud keeps us within the grip of pride. There's a lot of pride in that last sentence, but is this not indicative of our lives?

Pride comes in many packages. One of the greatest roots of pride is self-deception, or our inaccurate assessment of self. "If anyone thinks he is something when he is nothing, he deceives himself" (Galatians 6:3). Erin's view of her own competence was magnified. Yes, she had done a good job, but she failed to acknowledge that she was not immune to making a mistake. It's not unusual to think more highly of ourselves than we should. It's our nature to gravitate toward flattering comments.

As we allow an inflated view of self to continue, we start to distance ourselves from others. Our independence causes us to get larger, which pushes others away and makes them less in importance in our eyes. It's as if pride puts us in a balloon that's inflating, getting larger and larger, placing us farther away from others. We all know what happens to a balloon when it's blown up too big. Look out!

Distancing ourselves from others eventually causes us to have contempt for them. David wrote in the Psalms of his experience with the prideful: "Our life is exceedingly filled with the scorning and scoffing of those who are at ease and with the contempt of the proud—irresponsible tyrants who disregard God's law" (Psalm 123:4, AMP).

Erin had just started to entertain thoughts that maybe her boss wasn't needed. She felt she was as competent and knowledgeable as he was. Had she continued on that path, her disregard would have led to the point of feeling contempt toward him. This is particularly true in situations in which a boss or a coworker has to correct one of our mistakes or our behavior. Pride keeps us from seeing the truth about ourselves so as to avoid humiliation. We tend to be resistant to hearing a tough truth about ourselves and must guard against allowing ourselves to disrespect or even disdain those around us. Being attentive to these feelings of superiority can pinpoint the root of pride taking hold in our lives.

Sin does not lay dormant; it is always progressive in nature (see James 1:13-15). Pride is no different. Contempt will lead to oppression and a malicious spirit. "In his arrogance the wicked man hunts down the weak, who are caught in the schemes he devises" (Psalm 10:2) and "They scoff, and speak with malice; in their arrogance they threaten oppression" (Psalm 73:8). Contempt is an attitude of the heart. Oppression and malice are the outward actions that manifest the inner attitude. Maybe it starts with an attitude of superiority that dismisses the contributions of a junior associate on your team. Maybe it's a slight in the lunchroom about someone's character. Maybe it's an unwarranted negative evaluation. A heart full of pride will eventually evidence itself in actions.

A dangerous next step in pride and its effect on relationships is spiritual blindness.

When you have eaten and are satisfied . . . be careful that you do not forget the LORD your God, failing to observe his commands, his laws and his decrees that I am giving you this day. Otherwise, when you eat and are satisfied . . . then your heart will become proud and you will forget the LORD your God, who brought you out of Egypt, out of the land of slavery (*Deuteronomy 8:10-14*).

The Holy Spirit will warn us of the progressive nature of pride. But if we continually ignore the warning within our conscience, the natural outcome is that our hearts will become insensitive to His prompting. Our conscience will be dulled, and our hearts will be hardened. "There is no fear of God before his eyes. For in his own eyes he flatters himself too much to detect or hate his sin" (Psalm 36:1-2). This is a dangerous place to be, because the state of our hearts will always impact our relationships. "Above all else, guard your heart, for it is the wellspring of life" (Proverbs 4:23).

Corrective Measures

Some weeds in our gardens can be easily pulled, because their roots are shallow and weak. Others have a deep root system that must be dug up and treated with a strong chemical to ensure their demise. Pride seldom has a shallow root. It has been a part of humanity's relationships since the Fall. As such, the solution must be strong.

To counteract the erosive nature of pride on our relationships, we can ask God to develop within us an attitude of humility. Christ displayed the perfect example of humility when He set aside His privileges of deity and came to earth as a man, which culminated in His obedience to death on a cross (Philippians 2:3-4).

These corrective measures may not seem very powerful to you. You may be thinking, *Give me something to do. Make me a list of what I should and shouldn't do.* But that's the irony. We can't manufacture humility. Humility is not something to attain; rather, it's a state of heart. It's God who changes hearts. Have you ever found yourself thinking that you would be humble in a situation by hook or by crook? God will use our resolve to bring about change in our lives, but true humility is not formulated in our volition.

Two steps principally direct one's will. The first step is to admit that we have pride in our lives. "If we claim to be without sin, we deceive ourselves and the truth is not in us" (1 John 1:8). C. S. Lewis put it this way: "If anyone would like to acquire humility . . . tell him the first step. The first step is to realize that one is proud. And a biggish step, too. At least, nothing whatever can be done before it. If you think you are not conceited, it means you are very conceited indeed.[1]

The second step directs us to change our focus. If we are continually navel gazing, our attention is focused inward rather than upward or outward. If we go no further than trying to rid ourselves of pride, we will become even more narcissistic. Spend time with God. Read His words in Scripture, taking the time to ask the Holy Spirit to show you the relevance they have for you. It's imperative to have an open heart that allows God to pour into you. Have an open dialogue with Him throughout the day. You don't even have to pick up your cell phone to share the exciting development at work. Relish the fact that God is right there with you at your workplace.

As we get to know God personally and intimately, His presence brings to light the pride that we harbor. Just as infrared cameras detect the presence of life because of the warmth the body produces, so the Holy Spirit can detect the presence of pride in hearts. We may be so accustomed to this part of our character that we've become blind to it.

Thankfully, God is faithful to root out the sin in our lives and make us more like Him. I often think it would be nice if God would just do a major cleanout job—get rid of all the pride in my life; then I wouldn't have to worry about it anymore. Unfortunately, that's not how it works. Spiritual transformation is the gradual but continual process of Christ showing us where we need to detach from a way of life characterized by sin and attach to one that is more and more like Jesus.

Two steps: confess and focus. Sounds easy? I wish. Pride, characterized through self-deception, contempt, oppression, a malicious spirit, and a hardened heart, will tear relationships apart. The corrective measure of humility, not as we try to manufacture it but as it comes through a relationship with Christ, will build up and strengthen relationships.

Relationship Results

Relationships will crumble when pride takes root in our hearts. Haman thought he could manipulate the people in his life, but pride brought his demise. Erin thought she had everything under control, but pride brought her to her knees and jeopardized her workplace relationships. In order for our relationships to remain healthy and strong, we must be diligent to allow God, His Spirit, and His Word to root out pride.

The presence of God in Erin's life enabled her not only to identify her need to confess her pride to God but also to face the even more difficult task of apologizing to her boss. She knew she needed to meet with him face to face, acknowledge the error, and offer regret for the cocky attitude that led to it. Pride maintains an elevated view of ourselves, but we are warned against this. "Do not think of yourself more highly than you ought, but rather think of yourself with sober judgment" (Romans 12:3).

Humility provides a more accurate view of self. From that lessened and corrected view we'll have the courage to "confess [our] sins to each other and pray for each other so that [we] may be healed" (James 5:16).

Confession plays an integral part in rooting out pride and the flourishing of humility. Erin experienced the fall caused by pride, but she also tasted the sweetness of true humility that followed on the heels of humiliation. It was pride that had damaged the relational bridge and Christ-like humility that restored it.

Verses to Study

Genesis 3:1-5

1 John 1:8
Philippians 2:2, 4
Proverbs 11:2
Romans 12:3
Psalm 32:1, 2
Galatians 6:3
Proverbs 4:23
Daniel 4:37
Psalm 10:2-4

Questions for Reflection

1. How has pride caused you to view yourself more importantly than others? What actions have given evidence to this heart issue?

2. In what areas of life have you been trying to make life work without God?

3. What are you doing to allow God to point out pride in your life?

3 Deception Defeated by Integrity

Hannah's daughter was running late for school. Again. This happened far too frequently and often caused Hannah to be late for work. What excuse would she use today? She had already used all the good ones and was beginning to recycle them. She knew it was not her lucky day when she ran into her boss, Sandra, in the hall before she could get her coat off in her office.

"Hannah, I've been looking for you. I have to give an important update to the vice-president in five minutes. Where have you been—and where is the report on implementing the new software?" Sandra was quite firm.

"Oh, I'm sorry—I forgot about your nine o'clock meeting," said Hannah, thinking that her excuse had better be good to make up for letting Sandra down at such a critical point. "Our hot water tank broke last night, and the house was flooded this morning. It took the plumber forever to respond. I got here as fast as I could." *How could anyone not sympathize with that excuse?*

Sandra expressed her empathy for the mishap and stated that if Hannah needed to leave early to check on things at home, she could do so, but right now she needed a one-minute update on the new software implementation.

"Sure—I've received the vendor proposals, but our engineering services group has not yet provided final specifications. Unfortunately, there's going to be a two-week delay, and I don't know if we'll make the deadline." Hannah knew that it was really her lack of communication of a clear deadline that had caused the engineering group to be late.

"This is awful. The vice-president has demanded we have no more schedule slips. I'm going to take considerable heat for this. Thanks for the update." Sandra raced off to the boardroom. Hannah was thankful that she had once again survived a stressful situation. Some creative excuse-spinning had saved her skin again—or so she thought.

That afternoon Sandra and the human resources manager walked into Hannah's office, and the news wasn't good. It had come out in the morning meeting that Hannah was to blame for poorly communicating the project deadline to the engineering group. The vice-president wanted heads to roll, and the axe was closest to Sandra's and Hannah's necks. Then one of the other managers commented that he had seen and overheard Hannah that morning in the high school office dictating to the secretary the reason for her daughter's tardiness. "She said her daughter was late again because they had all slept in due to the drama class party that had gone late last night," said Mark, the business manager.

"Hannah, do you agree with or deny Mark's statement?" asked Sandra.

"Mark's statement is true," responded Hannah.

"I'm sorry, Hannah," Sandra said, "but we have no choice but to dismiss you with cause. There will be no severance package. I'll also let you know that I've been placed on probation by my supervisor for failing to properly manage this project."

Hannah hung her head to hide the shame and tears as she struggled to say, "I'm sorry."

How has deception become so engrained in the workplace? I believe there are five reasons that make us prone to an exaggerated or a diminutive portrayal of self. Psychology professor Robert Feldman is one of the world's leading authorities on deception, and his book *The Liar in Your Life* strongly influenced my thinking on this topic.

One of the most common and socially acceptable reasons we fudge the truth is to increase our likeability. Our ability to fit in socially, even in the workplace, is in large part dependent on our desire to avoid dissonance. Relationships tend to be built on commonalities, not differences. So in our attempt to find common ground, we distort our true opinions to mirror those of the person with whom we're speaking. Professor Feldman conducted a study that found that the average person lies three times every ten minutes in a conversation. The intention of these lies was not to manipulate. Rather, people lied so that they would come across as more interesting, likable, and desirable.[1]

We're afraid that we're just not nice enough for people to be interested in us as we are, so we beef up the truth about ourselves, hoping that there will be something in the exaggerated package that they'll find attractive.

Lying in the workplace also emanates from our fear that our competency is lagging, so we feel the need to project a better version of ourselves. Dallas Willard puts it this way:

When we're with those we feel less than secure with, we use words to "adjust" our appearance and elicit their approval. Otherwise we fear our virtues might not receive adequate appreciation and our shortcomings might not be properly understood.[2]

All too easily we succumb to our desire to enhance the perception others have of us by lying about our life story, inventing achievements, and inflating our career ambitions. Often there may be some nugget of truth, but it becomes embellished or downplayed—whichever makes us appear to have stronger skills or abilities. We anticipate that the true self we bring to the relationship will not be good enough. A desire to impress supersedes truthfulness.

Sometimes our reaction to a threatened ego can be the catalyst to lie. As we breeze in late to a top-of-the-morning meeting, we tell a "little white lie" as part of our apology for poor time management. The truth of the matter is that we stayed up too late reading a book and hit the snooze button three times. Maybe our boss asks if the task is nearing completion, and we say it is when, in fact, we've completed only twenty percent. Fear of the consequences causes us to create an altered reality smoke screen.

If each of these reasons for deception were increasingly destructive, this point would rank the highest: deception can be used to manipulate. Lies can be used as a tool to victimize or exploit people. When working on a team, Hannah failed to communicate an important deadline for the collection of information. When her boss came asking for the information, she quickly deferred the blame onto her coworkers who had not produced the necessary material. She victimized them by deceiving her boss and not owning her fault in the failure. The deception occurs through what's omitted and implied rather than blatant accusation.

Deception is a strategy of choice we use to achieve our motives of being liked, looking competent, protecting ourselves, or manipulating others for our own gain. Just as mold grows rapidly in dark places, so does our propensity and need to continue leading a life of deception. One lie is seldom enough.

Hannah had choices to make when she met her boss in the hallway. She could be honest about a problem she was having at home or lie to make it sound better. She could be honest about her mistake in project deadline communication or falsely shift blame. Hannah's responses and her situation weren't the product of a one-time slip of lying. Lying was a habit she had developed that compounded her trouble.

Deception has a huge effect on relationships. Hannah paid a price for the web of lies she was caught in that day. Let's suppose that she had not been fired that day and had been given a second chance. She would have lived under the weight of trying to rebuild trust with Sandra, the rest of the management team, and the engineering group, and all of them would have known about her dishonesty. That's a much greater burden to bear than having to come clean about her actions and take responsibility for them.

Rebuilding damaged trust is a monumental task. It takes many more demonstrations of trustworthiness to rebuild relational bridges that have been damaged by deception than it takes to maintain them.

The choice is whether or not we'll allow deception to enter our relationship with God and others despite the disastrous effect it may have on them—or choose to be honest, knowing that this will bode best for us in the long run and enable us to build strong relational bridges with others.

Corrective Measures

If deception is telling and living a life of lies, then honesty is behavior that conveys truth regardless of the consequences. The corrective measure that must be used against the erosive power of deception is a commitment to stay on the narrow path of honesty. Remember the initial key verse of loving God, ourselves, and others? Honesty is an integral part of this. Scripture says that God desires truth in the inner parts (Psalm 51:6). He desires for us to have "truth from the inside out" (Psalm 51:6, TM).

We seem often to forget that our omniscient God sees everything, hears our inner thoughts, and understands the motives of our hearts. We don't have to come clean for Him to know what's going on inside us; but He also realizes the tremendous benefit to us when we're honest with Him. The only way to break the cycle of deception is to be honest with ourselves and with God.

Too often we shy away from confession—even to God—because of shame and the fear of not being accepted. I think of the story of Hosea and his adulterous wife, Gomer. She repeatedly left her husband to revert to her adulterous lifestyle, but Hosea went looking for her and kept bringing her back. He was full of love and forgiveness for Gomer.

Hosea lived this reality to portray to us God's view of us. We may continue to return to deception, but God keeps extending an olive branch of grace that says, "I want you back." Let's not allow our shame to keep us from coming back into a right relationship with God. Responding to the Holy Spirit's prompting to confess our sin to God will be the first step in breaking the bondage of this sin in our lives.

We're also told to love ourselves. How do you feel when you've just told a lie? Initially I may feel euphoria at having gotten away with it. However, in the quietness of the night and in the depth of my soul, I must face the fact that I've betrayed myself. I know that I really am not who I've portrayed myself to be. At that point I struggle with disgust toward my own deceptive actions and my pitiful reality. I realize that deceptive actions that I use to try to pump up my reality are hurting only me and certainly do not convey true love for myself. If I truly loved the woman God made me to be, I would be content in the authentic representation of myself.

The third part of Christ's ultimate command from Matthew is to love others. Loving the people we work with demands that we live a life of honesty. Shading the truth to save our own skin puts others at risk. To make this relational bridge stronger, we can give the gift of authenticity. Authenticity is sharing the gift of my true self. It demands putting aside games, roles I play, or pretending.

Being genuine does not mean communicating everything I feel or think. But it does mean that what I do communicate, I genuinely feel, believe, and think.[3]

Imagine how authenticity could strengthen and encourage mutual disclosure if we allowed people to really get to know who we are.

You may have read that last statement and be thinking, *My relationships are a lot better based on the person I've created at work rather than the real me.* Thoughts like these do not come from God.

Listen to what God says: "This is what you must do: Tell the truth to each other. Render verdicts in your courts that are just and that lead to peace. Don't scheme against each other. Stop your love of telling lies that you swear are the truth. I hate all these things" (Zechariah 8:16-17). If we're committed to building relational bridges God's way, then we must give up deception and live a new life of honesty and authenticity.

Taking Honesty a Step Further

Honesty is living truthfully, and *authenticity* is being genuine, but integrity includes and goes beyond both of these.

The origins of the word we can see in French and Latin meanings of *intact, integrate, integral, and entirety*. The concept means that the "whole thing is working well, undivided, integrated, intact, and uncorrupted." When we talk about integrity, we are talking about being a whole person, an integrated person, with all of our different parts working well and delivering the functions that they were designed to deliver. It is about wholeness and effectiveness as people.[4]

Integrity is keeping promises and fulfilling expectations.[5] This leads to freedom and a milieu in which relationships are strengthened.

Children often lie to get themselves out of sticky situations; adults tend to display the same immature traits by simply making more intricate lies. Integrity calls greatness out of us and gives evidence of our maturity as a person. The writer of Hebrews gives an indication of a mature person's ability to make decisions. "Solid food is for those who are mature, who through training have the skill to recognize the difference between right and wrong" (Hebrews 5:14). Integrity will develop through practice and will evidence itself as the ability to decipher right from wrong and then pursue it.

In the workplace we must start with honesty and then add authenticity, realizing our character culminates with integrity. Hannah's integrity started to erode when she told her first lie about why she was late for work. For fear of being considered incompetent for allowing home issues to affect her work, she chose to portray herself as an efficient woman who had it all together. She was no longer presenting her genuine self, and to maintain this facade she had to conjure a scenario that would support her deception. Integrity is a high calling and demands dependence on an even higher standard set by God. Our ability to live a life of integrity will topple if the base of honesty and authenticity is not present.

The Story of Esther

How did Esther live a life of integrity? Some might argue that she lived a lie by not divulging her Jewish heritage to the king when she became queen. It's difficult to understand why Mordecai told Esther not to reveal her heritage when it was known in Mordecai's circles that he was a Jew. Looking back, we can see the plan God had for Esther's life that would impact the survival of His people. From Esther's example we can draw the principle that we may not have to tell everything about ourselves, but when the opportunity and prompting comes to be authentic, we must trust God's timing and obey His call to authenticity. Esther displayed a life of integrity by risking her life when she revealed she was a Jew. When her people needed her, she had the courage to put aside her self-protection.[6]

Relationship Results

Relational bridges are built on the foundation of love and trust. Deception will have a tremendous eroding effect. God has called us to live lives characterized by truth. If we choose to do otherwise, we'll reap what we sow, and our relationships will suffer. The last verses of the Book of Hosea are these:

If you want to live well, make sure you understand all of this. If you know what's good for you, you'll learn this inside and out. God's paths get you where you want to go. Right-living people walk them easily; wrong-living people are always tripping and stumbling *(Hosea 14:9, TM)*.

In our efforts to build relational bridges in the workplace, we can build strong bridges by living lives of honesty, authenticity, and integrity. If we engage in deception, the bridge will break down. The choice is God's way or our way.

Verses to Study

Psalm 51:6
Hosea 14:9
Proverbs 11:3
1 Peter 2:1-3
Proverbs 26:28
Ephesians 4:15
Proverbs 6:16-19
Hebrews 5:14
Zechariah 8:16-17

Questions for Reflection

1. When have you felt the need to embellish the truth or outright lie to be seen as acceptable at work?

2. Describe a time when you experienced the weight of having to rebuild trust in a relationship after it was broken by dishonesty.

3. Are you living a life of integrity at work? What do you need to change so that you're presenting your complete self—physically, emotionally, mentally, and spiritually—at work?

4 Anger Diffused by Forgiveness

"I'm so angry!"

"I'm spittin' mad!"

"If she crosses me one more time, I'll no longer be responsible for my actions!"

"Anger is a feeling of outrage or indignation against either an injustice or an insult."[1] It's often conceived justifiably: a coworker produces shoddy work, and we're left to pick up the pieces; a boss takes his frustration out on us minutes after his boss has raked him over the coals; a customer blames us for the breakage of the product when we're simply the salesperson. All these are examples of injustices perpetrated upon us. Becoming angry about these things is neither unnatural nor wrong, but it's the action that comes out of anger that becomes the problem. Before we explore the typical next steps in the development of anger, let's examine anger that wells out of deep hurts.

It had just been announced that Melanie was the recipient of the Employee of the Month award. Character qualities of integrity, hard work, and compassion had been noted in the announcement released by Human Resources. Melanie felt humbled that her co-workers and management had viewed her work as exemplary and had bestowed this honor on her.

As she sat reading the congratulatory e-mail that flooded her desktop, one arrived from Meg, a woman Melanie worked with a number of years earlier. She opened it with anticipation, but as she read the few short lines, enthusiasm turned to feeling as though her heart had been pierced and life was pouring out. Rather than reading a note of congratulations, Melanie read words that slammed her character and discredited her work. Someone she thought was a longtime ally had stabbed her in the heart. Disbelief turned to anger.

Did Melanie have the right to be angry about this e-mail? Many very nice women would probably say no.

Studies of children's play show boys competing (both physically and verbally) and fighting. Girls tend to play cooperatively; they work hard to resolve differences. Women also grow up maintaining relationships at almost any cost. . . . We try desperately not to rock the boat.[2]

This is even more pronounced in the Christian community, where many of us have heard that getting angry is wrong. You may find yourself thinking, *Wait a minute here. This really hurt my feelings. Don't my feelings count?*

Jesus was not void of anger. He often expressed His anger toward the Pharisees and religious leaders as their hardened hearts pierced His heart (Mark 3:5). He became angry when He discovered the Temple being used as a marketplace (John 2:15). Many times in the Old Testament God became angry at the sins of the stubborn Israelites. Anger is a God-given emotion. We have the ability to feel, because we're created as emotional beings in the image of God (Genesis 1:27). Anger is one of the most powerful emotions. However, it must follow the proper channel, or it becomes destructive.

Negative Channels

When Melanie received the e-mail, she could have fired back a sarcastic response that noted the obvious reason that Meg had never been chosen for the award. She could have picked up the knife that had been thrown at her and thrown it back to wound her offender. Then she could have begun to bad-mouth Meg around the office by telling others the unbelievable comments Meg had made.

More subversively, Melanie could have decided she was going to avoid Meg at all cost. She could retreat with her anger, but then every time Melanie encountered Meg, her pulse would rise, and the fear of future interactions would become paralyzing. If she chose this path of passive-aggressive behavior, it would take considerable energy to maintain the needed manipulation of her work environment in order to avert further contact with Meg.

Melanie could have acknowledged the hurt caused by Meg's statements and then pretended to move on with life. Outwardly, everything would seem fine, but in her own mind and heart Melanie would continue to pick at the wound. When sorting through old e-mail, she would come across the flagged message from Meg and reread it. This common occurrence would refuel her justification to keep bitterness tucked away in her heart.

All these options would have taken Melanie down a path where her initial anger would lead to sin. Slander, disengagement, and a lack of forgiveness are all eroding factors in relationships. None of these options would take us down the path of living as Jesus told us to live and certainly would not lead to healthy relationships.

Is there another way?

Corrective Measures

If anyone has ever told you the best way to stop anger is to simply refuse to be angry, you probably wanted to kick her. Such a circular argument only leads to defeat and frustration. The solution to anger is not to simply stop being angry. Anger *will* happen. The corrective measure lies in the way we respond to anger. Neglecting to acknowledge our anger and the resulting hurt typically means that we hold onto that emotion deep down. Eventually it surfaces—often against someone other than the person who caused of it. In speaking of the role of our emotions with respect to spiritual transformation, Dallas Willard says that "[Emotions] more than any other component of our nature are the 'triggers' of sinful action."[3] For example, you end up blowing up at your child over dinner when she talks with food in her mouth, when the real issue is the anger you allowed to accumulate over the past week toward your coworker.

One of the most poignant and instructive verses in Scripture on anger is Ephesians 4:26-27: "Go ahead and be angry. You do well to be angry—but don't use your anger as fuel for revenge. And don't stay angry. Don't go to bed angry. Don't give the Devil that kind of foothold in your life" (TM). This reiterates that there are times and situations when anger is justified. But the latter part of those verses lays out two criteria that will keep us from crossing that line into sin territory.

Don't Let It Grow

The first checkpoint to keep anger from becoming sinful is that we must not allow it to become fuel for revenge.

Brenda had been placed in the situation of having to spend the weekend at the office to finish up a project because her coworker Tina, who passed the data on to her, had been late. Now Brenda was cramming to get the presentation ready for Monday morning.

As she sat at her desk on a sunny Saturday afternoon, she could feel the emotional temperature rising in her spirit. Come Monday morning, Brenda's appearance was cool and collected, but on the inside she was steaming. She opted to give no evidence of being disgruntled.

As the weeks passed, Brenda found herself avoiding Tina, because every time she thought about that lost weekend she felt anger rising and morphing into bitterness. Her boss had suggested that Brenda and Tina work together on another project, but Brenda quickly manufactured an excuse as to why she wasn't available to do that. Brenda realized she was entertaining negative thoughts toward her boss as well, because he evidently admired Tina's work. She wondered how anyone could be that blind to Tina's incompetence. Brenda looked for ways to get even with Tina.

It was easy not to pass on to others the materials Tina funneled through her, but Brenda soon progressed to subtlety, alluding to Tina's incompetence when speaking with coworkers. It was not that the initial anger Brenda felt had been wrong—it was that Brenda had held it in and allowed it to grow into bitterness and revenge. Brenda would have been able to nip her anger if she had gone to Tina when the problem first arose and explained to her the negative effects that her tardiness was having. Had she been able to put proper boundaries in place to minimize the chance of it happening again, the anger would not have festered.

Matthew 18 lays out a process for dealing with relational discourse:

> If a fellow believer hurts you, go and tell him—work it out between the two of you. If he listens, you've made a friend. If he won't listen, take one or two others along so that the presence of witnesses will keep things honest, and try again. If he still won't listen, tell the church. If he won't listen to the church, you'll have to start over from scratch, confront him with the need for repentance, and offer again God's forgiving love (*Matthew 18:15-17, TM*).

Usually if this process is engaged with honesty and humility, it will reap a mutual apology and a restoration of the relationship. Unfortunately, the underlying desire of one or both parties may not be mutual apology and mutual forgiveness but rather sole superiority of one party over the other.

Uncommon Forgiveness

Forgiveness is a most common word—but a most uncommon practice. If we've entered into a personal relationship with Jesus Christ, then we're the recipients of His divine forgiveness of our sins. On the basis of the once-for-all sacrifice offered by Jesus Christ on the Cross, God has wiped away our sin when we come to Him in repentance. His forgiveness means that my sins are forgotten and are no longer held against me. "I will forgive their wickedness and will remember their sins no more" (Jeremiah 31:34). God's endless grace and mercy to us are evidenced through His forgiveness. In doing so, God built and maintains the ultimate relational bridge to us. He handed us the olive branch of forgiveness so that we could be in relationship.

This should make it easy for us to pass that forgiveness on to the people who have hurt us, but too often it doesn't work that way. In glossing over the fact that we're guilty and in need of forgiveness, we choose instead to find fault with how others have treated us badly, hold grudges, and fuel anger into bitterness and revenge. Refusing to forgive as we have been forgiven contravenes the Lord's Prayer—"Forgive our debts as we have also forgiven our debtors" (Matthew 6:12).

Jesus tells a parable about a servant who owed today's equivalent of millions of dollars to the king. Unable to pay his debt, he begged for mercy from the king who granted a stay, cancelling his debt and letting the servant go. No sooner had this servant been released from his own chains of debt than he went looking for a fellow servant who had owed him a few dollars. He grabbed him by the neck, attempting to choke him, demanding that he repay his meager debt. When the debtor refused, the servant had him thrown into prison until he could pay back these few dollars (Matthew 18:21-35).

It is no mistake that this parable of the unforgiving servant follows the Matthew 18 process of how to work out relational strife. If the scenario plays out that the offender repents, then offering forgiveness is much easier. But if the offender maintains his or her innocence and instead places the fault on us, God's supernatural forgiveness still reminds us of our need to forgive. We cannot do this on our own, but since God has modeled for us and strengthened us with the Holy Spirit, we do have this gift within us, ready to spill out. "Bear with each other and forgive whatever grievances you may have against one another. Forgive as the Lord forgave you" (Colossians 3:13).

What does it mean to forgive someone? A visual that has made this real to me is that of unleashing ourselves from the person who has hurt us. This means that the two of us are no longer tied together by our infraction. Imagine being tethered to a wild tiger. Would you not do everything within your power to unleash yourself from the imminent harm a tiger could do?

Yet we do it all the time. We keep ourselves tied to the memories of cutting remarks, wrongful dismissals, bypassed promotions, backstabbing and gossip, and fractured relationships. In so doing, we keep ourselves tethered to a dangerous animal that has the potential to deplete our soul. This can manifest itself as exhaustion, defeat, or anger and a desire for revenge. As a writer who suffered childhood abuse reflected, "I've found that forgiveness adds to my quality of life. . . not that I have attained perfection in it, but I have proved I am the worse for not doing it!"[4]

Forgiveness occurs when we allow God to cut the tether to free us from the effects of the wound. Even eighteen months after receiving the slamming e-mail, Melanie realized that she had been picking at the scab of that wound, and it continued to cause damage to her soul. In desperation, she cried out to God to help her forgive, to help her let go of the hurt. Jesus has promised that He would move into our weakness and give us the power we need to forgive. "My grace is sufficient for you, for my power is made perfect in weakness" (2 Corinthians 12:9).

Seven Times?

Have you noticed that anger tends to resurface in your heart? Sometimes I think I've dealt with a certain situation—then something refreshes the memory, and I again find myself needing to offer forgiveness. I think this is why the Ephesians passage ends with the warning not to let the devil get "that kind of foothold" on our lives. If we open the door and entertain anger, sin moves in. Listen to the warning that God gives to Cain, who is livid that his brother Abel had received God's favor: "If you do what is right, will you not be accepted? But if you do not do what is right, sin is crouching at your door; it desires to have you, but you must master it" (Genesis 4:7). We must continue to deal with the anger that lurks at the door of our hearts and minds.

I find it fascinating that in the Lord's Prayer the request for forgiveness follows the request for daily bread. Could the two be connected?[5] Could our need for daily sustenance be as primal as our need to receive and offer forgiveness? I know I don't feel physically well when I go too long without food. Nor do I enjoy emotional health when I allow unforgiveness to accumulate. Just as we'll require food every day, so will we need to receive God's forgiveness and extend forgiveness to others from now until the day we die.

Perhaps it's this daily connection that prompted Jesus to respond to Peter's question about how many times it's necessary to forgive (Matthew 18:21). No doubt Peter thought he was being pretty spiritual if he was willing to forgive the same offense seven times. Jewish tradition taught that it was "presumptuous and unnecessary to forgive anyone more than three times."[6] Jesus' response—"Peter, try seventy times seven" (Matthew 18:22)—was not meant to limit forgiveness to a specific number but rather to make the point that our forgiveness should be endless.

Forgiveness is an endlessly tough road.

God Redeems

God has an amazing way of taking the tough stuff that happens to us and reversing it so that something good comes of it. It's called redemption. The actual meaning of redemption is the buying-back or release of someone or something. How does it work? God takes the hurt caused by the insult or slander and redeems it so that rather than our anger leading us into sin, it brings glory to Him. Let me give you an example from Scripture.

Many bad things happened to Joseph. His brothers sold him into slavery; then his master's wife falsely accused him of rape, which landed him in prison for seven years. These occurrences were certainly enough to justify Joseph's anger. But God had His hand on Joseph. Instead of his heart being full of bitterness and a desire for revenge, his pain was redeemed. This is how Joseph described to his brothers what had happened in his heart: "You intended to harm me, but God intended it for good to accomplish what is now being done, the saving of many lives (Genesis 50:20).

The apostle Paul also had every right to be angry as he sat in a prison cell in Philippi. Instead, he chose to view it this way: "My imprisonment here has had the opposite of its intended effect" (Philippians 1:12, TM). Redemption is God taking the ugly and making something beautiful.

All of us have experienced the actions or words of another that have hurt us deeply and resulted in the emotion of anger within us. At that juncture, each of us makes the choice of what to do with the anger. Will it prompt us to go and make amends with the person, or will it cause us to retreat and plot revenge? Will it cause us to lash out in bitterness in an attempt to hurt the other person as much as he or she hurt us? Or will we follow the example of Christ as He hung precariously between life and death, His body brutally beaten, yet offered forgiveness to His tormentors? The choice we make will either free us from the chains that hold us to the offense or will continue to rip us apart. "When a soul loves and forgives, it soars to freedom on wings like an eagle's. But a soul bound to revenge and bitterness sinks to the depths of the sea and lives forever bound by the ties of self."[7]

King Solomon said it this way: "When you're kind to others, you help yourself; when you're cruel to others, you hurt yourself" (Proverbs 11:17, TM).

Old anger resurfaces, and new anger develops. It will always be with us, but we must not sin in our anger. It is forgiveness that will build the bridge to our coworkers. You may be thinking, *I have tried to build a relationship with that person, but every time I do, the bridge gets sabotaged.*

If we follow the relational process laid out in Matthew 18 and live by the verse "If it is possible, as far as it depends on you, live at peace with everyone" (Romans 12:18), there may still be certain people with whom a bridge cannot be maintained. We cannot force ourselves on others, but we can know that in our hearts we harbor nothing against them. Forgiveness is a one-way street; restoration is a two-way street. Should the other person show a desire for a relationship, we should be willing and ready to recommit to the work involved in building a bridge to restore the relationship. Let's be quick to forgive so that anger does not drain our souls of the joy God has placed there through His forgiveness of us.

The Esther Connection

As in every person's chronicle, the story of Esther has an underlying subplot of anger. King Xerxes had thrown a lavish party for his military leaders and nobles that showcased his wealth and splendor. As a pinnacle to this event, he summoned his queen to come and display her beauty to her guests. When she refused, "The king became furious and burned with anger" (Esther 2:12). It was in his wrath that Xerxes made the decree that Vashti would never again enter his presence, and thus she was stripped of her royal position. Scripture goes on to say that "Later when the anger of King Xerxes had subsided, he remembered Vashti and what she had done and what he had decreed about her" (Esther 2:1). I can't help but wonder as Xerxes contemplated what he had done, if he had some degree of remorse for his hasty decision. Decisions made in anger are often unwise.

Later in the story, Haman received an invitation to join Esther and the king for a banquet. Despite leaving the palace feeling rather buoyed, he became filled with rage when Mordecai neither rose nor showed fear of him (Esther 5:9). It was this burning wrath that fueled Haman's choice to erect gallows to destroy his enemy. In the end, his anger became the fuel for his own demise.

Verses to Study

Ephesians 4:26-27
Matthew 18:15-17, 21-35
Jeremiah 31:33-34
Matthew 6:9-13
Colossians 3:12-14
Philippians 1:12
Romans 12:17-21
Genesis 4:7
2 Corinthians 12:9-10
Proverbs 11:12, 17

Questions for Reflection

1. Can you identify times you have pursued some of the negative channels for anger described in this chapter?

2. What hurtful memories are you continuing to mull over and thus remain tied to?

3. Describe a situation or a relationship that's in need of the daily bread of forgiveness. What causes you to be miserly with your forgiveness?

5 Judgment Dissolved by Grace

He was late again. Julie checked her watch. Her colleague, who had just passed her door, briefcase in hand, slinked into work an hour later than the rest of the department. She decided to follow him as he headed toward the coffee station. She wanted to discreetly assess his situation. She shook her head with disgust at his wrinkled clothes and disheveled hair. *Didn't he care enough about his job to at least put on fresh clothes in the morning? Had he ever heard of an iron?*

When he looked up to greet her, she saw the large puffy bags under his bloodshot eyes. She wondered at which bar he had spent the night. He was a perfect example of a respectable drunk trying to hold down a day job.

As Julie strode back to her office, she passed the woman whose office was across the hall and five doors down. In an ideal world she should not have been able to hear anything that was said in this woman's office, but because of her loud and screechy voice, Julie and the rest of the department could hear almost every word. *Why did she have to be so loud? Why did she get so quiet when she saw me? She must be talking about me. She's probably the source of that gossip that's been spreading about me. I knew she couldn't be trusted.*

Back in her office Julie had just sat down at her desk when her telephone rang and she answered. The boss's secretary asked her to come immediately to the executive's office.

Julie said she would be right there, but as she grabbed her Blackberry, she couldn't help but wonder what the slave-driver wanted this time. The last time she had been called into his office, she had been reprimanded for a slight misdemeanor on her current project. Tough as it was, the issue was dealt with effectively, and three weeks of calm had passed. Now she was being summoned again to the office. She couldn't think of any contraventions she would be guilty of, but then she had been ignorant of the first misdemeanor until confronted. She was sure her boss had it in for her, and this latest summons would likely confirm it. Who knows? Maybe she was going to be handed a pink slip! This boss had seemed malicious—even sadistic—right from the beginning. This couldn't be good.

Within an hour of coming to work, Julie had allowed assumptions and judgments to create a distance between her and two of her coworkers and her boss. Her propensity to judge people's intentions, motives, or actions—not based on fact but on assumptions—created a relational chasm between her and her coworkers.

Do You See the Issue?

I worked in an office setting that was designed around the open-air concept. We each had our own cubicle that rose a meager four feet off the ground. We sat huddled in our own corner trying to not disturb the people around us. I tend to talk to myself as I'm writing, so every so often someone would poke his or her head over my cubicle wall with an inquisitive look, wondering to whom I was talking. I would simply smile and say, "Sorry, just talking to myself. I'll try to keep it down."

Despite being annoying to others, I had no problem being judgmental of those I worked alongside. There was the coworker whose booming voice jerked me out of my concentration. *Why couldn't he lower his voice a few decibels?* There was the person who had a peculiar gait, and her clicking high heels distracted me. *Why couldn't she wear flats?* Then I discovered that the person who shared my cubicle had a nasty head cold. She came to work and sneezed all over the hardware on our desks. It gave a whole new meaning to "catching a computer virus." *Why couldn't she have stayed home for a day or two and kept her germs to herself?* I would have shown that courtesy to her.

I realized my thought patterns were all mixed up. I was quick to judge my coworkers' motives and actions, and in doing so I came across as exemplary in my own view. In short order, self-elevating thoughts developed: *I would never do that. I'm better, I'm smarter, and I'm definitely more considerate than them.*

Assumptions are made for a number of reasons. It's quicker and easier to make a judgment than it is to investigate. We also make assumptions because some of us have natural bent to imagine the worst about others, passing judgment on them and thereby elevating ourselves. Someone who is hypocritical easily shifts the responsibility for making changes onto another. If we can assume the other person is the villain or the one in need of help, then the scale will tip against them, and we'll come out—at least in our opinion—looking just that much better. It's easiest to assume the other person is at fault and ignore the role we play in the situation. We must recognize that our heart is bent toward protecting and elevating ourselves, even at the expense of another.

I love to take risks, seek adventure, and get things done. I often become frustrated when I work alongside someone who's a thinker, planner, and more laid back. Insidiously, I begin to think that my personality is better than the other person's and that my strengths contribute more. I become very self-focused and self-celebratory in my heart while becoming critical of the other person. I no longer see the strengths of his or her personality, seeing him or her instead as too slow to make decisions, too methodical, too quiet, too unlike me. In simple terms, I'm superior—the other person has the problems.

You don't have to be a psychologist with a lot of letters after your name to figure out what this does to relationships. The Adam legacy of relating, "I'll celebrate myself and judge you," fractures relationships.[1] Even just harboring these thoughts in my heart causes the fracture. Our hearts are the wellspring of life (Proverbs 4:23), so when there's sin in our hearts, it will eventually spill out. My desire to "encourage" change so that my coworkers could become more like me, not more like Christ, pushed them away and caused the chasm between us to widen. The writer of Romans had this to say: "Every time you criticize someone, you condemn yourself. It takes one to know one. Judgmental criticism of others is a well-known way of escaping detection in your own crimes and misdemeanors" (Romans 2:2, TM).

Corrective Measures

Jesus was in the middle of an ordinary workday. He had spent the night praying, selected the twelve men who would form His inner team for the next three years, and then spent the day healing the people who swarmed around Him. After all this chaos, He turned to His disciples and began to talk to them about what was really important in the kingdom of heaven.

This "Sermon on the Mount" focuses in large part on relationships. Part-way through, Jesus makes this statement: "Here's a simple rule of thumb for behavior" (Luke 6:31, TM). Jesus walks us through the Golden Rule and the importance of loving others. Little by little, He comes closer to the bull's-eye of the problem until He uses a metaphor that pinpoints it in our relationships: "Why do you look at the speck of sawdust in your brother's eye and pay no attention to the plank in your own eye? How can you say to your brother, 'Brother, let me take the speck out of your eye,' when you yourself fail to see the plank in your own eye? You hypocrite, first take the plank out of your eye, and then you will see clearly to remove the speck from your brother's eye" (Luke 6:41-42).

In true Jesus style, He doesn't beat around the bush; He *tells* us what is wrong. We've become so obsessed with what's wrong with others and their need to fix it that we have no time or energy left to work on the problems that hinder us. Think for a minute about the metaphor that Jesus uses. The person across from you has a speck in his or her eye. Specks are annoying and cause irritation, but they're not life-threatening. Planks can cause permanent, irreparable damage. Planks are more than an inconvenience—they're critical. Given these two scenarios—speck and plank—which needs to be dealt with?

Christ tells us that we need to quit looking for the speck in someone else's eye and take care of the plank in our own. In essence, what He's saying is that we need to stop making judgments that are often based on assumptions. Our roles in life are not to be watchful for the faults in others, but rather we're to soberly look at our own shortcomings. When we're aware of the plank in our own lives, we won't worry about the speck in the lives of others.

Investigation and Empathy

There's a very good reason that God has given us two eyes and two ears—but only one mouth. We're to take in more than we give out by using our eyes and ears to gather information from multiple sources. We need to have the ears and eyes of Jesus and become involved in people's lives so that we can see and understand their circumstances.

Empathy is a corrective measure that will have a pronounced positive impact on relationships. When we empathize, we identify with and understand the other person's situation. This takes time and effort, as opposed to mounting the judgment seat and assuming we know everything. Making assumptions can take us down many paths, but asking for clarification, trying to understand what has happened in people's lives, and listening for their perspective will create an opportunity for empathy rather than judgment. There is great wisdom in the old saying "Before you judge someone, walk a mile in his shoes." During that mile we can learn much about the person's life, struggles, experience, and present situation.

People who make assumptions tend to ask few questions. Having already made up their minds, they would rather think they're right than search for evidence that might contradict their position. People who give the gift of empathy ask questions, listen, learn, and give the benefit of the doubt. They remain open to understanding rather than being quick to judge. Open questions such as "This is what I see—can you help me understand what's going on in your life?" have a much different effect on relationships than closed statements such as "This is what you're like, and now you need to deal with that."

I find it instructive that Jesus, God Incarnate, who knew everything about each person around Him, chose to ask questions. Why did the all-knowing God bother to investigate? I believe it's because Jesus knew that good questions can be the impetus for transformation. Questions draw people into relationship.

Extend Grace

There will be situations that will require us to make judgments as to whether something is right or wrong. I'm not suggesting that we should avoid taking a stand against wrong. But when we have to make difficult decisions, we should do it out of a heart that desires restoration. Christ had an interaction with a woman who had been caught in sin and was guilty according to the law. She had a plank— but Jesus extended grace to her.

The story is retold in *The Message,* John 8:1-11:

Jesus went across to Mount Olives, but he was soon back in the Temple again. Swarms of people came to him. He sat down and taught them. The religion scholars and Pharisees led in a woman who had been caught in an act of adultery. They stood her in plain sight of everyone and said, "Teacher, this woman was caught red-handed in the act of adultery. Moses, in the Law, gives orders to stone such persons. What do you say?" They were trying to trap him into saying something incriminating so they could bring charges against him.

Jesus bent down and wrote with his finger in the dirt. They kept at him, badgering him. He straightened up and said, "The sinless one among you, go first: Throw the stone." Bending down again, he wrote some more in the dirt.

Hearing that, they walked away, one after another, beginning with the oldest. The woman was left alone. Jesus stood up and spoke to her. "Woman, where are they? Does no one condemn you?"

"No one, Master."

"Neither do I," said Jesus. "Go on your way. From now on, don't sin."

Jesus, the sinless Son of God, had every right to condemn her, based not on assumption but by the facts that were presented to Him. But as is so characteristic of God's character, *grace* was extended to this woman. I wonder what we would do if we had been Jesus that day. Would we have chosen judgment over grace?

Certainly there are times when we have to make tough decisions, but imagine what would develop in our relationships if we traded assumptions, evaluation, and judgments for empathy, investigation, and grace. The Golden Rule directs us to treat others the way we want to be treated. Scripture says that the entire law is summed up in "Love your neighbor as yourself" (Galatians 5:14). We can make assessments about the things people are doing and slam them with the law—but never show them love.

When you love others, you complete what the law has been after all along. The law code—don't sleep with another person's spouse, don't take someone's life, don't take what isn't yours, don't always be wanting what you don't have, and any other "don't" you can think of—finally adds up to this: Love other people as well as you do yourself. You can't go wrong when you love others. When you add up everything in the law code, the sum total is love *(Romans 13:8-10, TM)*.

The relational bridge between God and us is built on love that evidences itself by God's extending grace to us. "While we were yet sinners, Christ died for us" (Romans 5:8). All of us are guilty. None of us is deserving of God's grace, but He still gives it. By definition, grace is the giving of underserved favor. Grace, whether it's God extending it to us or we're extending it to others, is always unmerited. "For just as all the streamlets that flow from a clear spring are as clear as the spring itself, so the works of a soul in grace are pleasing in the eyes both of God and of men."[2]

The Story of Esther

In the brief account of Esther's life, there's much we're not told. We are not given a glimpse into how she felt during her first night with the king nor the emotions she experienced as she was taken from Mordecai to enter the king's harem. There's much we could assume about these situations. Rather, let's simply look at times when Esther refused to make assumptions and instead investigated the reality of situations. It was this information that enabled her to make decisions based on fact rather than assumption.

Esther was living in the enclave of the palace at Susa. As a woman living in that time, she would have had greater independence than is evidenced by many women living today in the Mideastern regions of the world. It was common, particularly for royal women, to have "economic independence, (to be) involved in the administration of economic affairs, and to travel and control their wealth and position by being active, resolute, and enterprising."[3] But the affairs of the kingdom would have been dealt with by the king and his nobles. Consequently, it would have been reasonable for Esther to be unaware of the edict that had been issued to annihilate the Jewish people. The king might not have discussed such affairs with her. She was dependent on news trickling into the palace from other sources.

Mordecai, on the other hand, was in the thick of things. He worked within the king's court as a scribe and lived out in the community where he further received news. Upon hearing the devastating announcement, he "tore his clothes, put on sackcloth and ashes, and went out into the city, wailing loudly and bitterly" (Esther 4:1). Mordecai's actions soon were made known to Esther, and she became greatly distressed at his behavior. What could have happened that caused Mordecai to go into mourning? Had someone close to their family died? Had he lost favor with the court and been expelled? Had his reputation or that of their family been tarnished?

Esther did not waste her time making assumptions. Rather, she sought clarification by sending out one of her attending eunuchs to discover the reason behind his actions. Imagine if Esther had assumed that Mordecai was simply playing one of the many required ritualistic roles of their culture of if she had been paralyzed by the fears that her imagination could have spawned. Either way, Esther was now in a position to make choices that would impact her and the people around her, especially if she did not seek to investigate the truth, however good or bad the truth might have been.

Relationship Results

Julie recounts that it was learning of the true situation of her disheveled coworker that finally broke through her propensity for making judgments and showed her how they negatively affected her relationships.

He had not been out on a drunken binge. He had just come from the hospital where he had spent the entire night sitting by his mother's bedside as she struggled with each breath through the latter stages of a debilitating disease. Her usually noisy office neighbor had gone silent because she had been planning a surprise team-building event, not because she was talking about Julie. Julie's boss didn't intend to give her a warning or hand her a pink slip; he wanted to thank her for the improvements he was seeing in the quality of her work. When Julie realized how far off the mark she had been about her workplace situations, she began to wonder where she had made assumptions and judgments in other relationships.

A similar example is described in Scripture:

My dear friends, don't let public opinion influence how you live out our glorious, Christ-originated faith. If a man enters your church wearing an expensive suit, and a street person wearing rags comes in right after him, and you say to the man in the suit, "Sit here, sir; this is the best seat in the house!" and either ignore the street person or say, "Better sit here in the back row," haven't you segregated God's children and proved that you are judges who can't be trusted?" (*James 2:2-4, TM*).

Just as a hailstone starts with a speck of dust at the core and then layer upon layer of water collects and freezes, so assumptions may start with a speck of reality. Our imaginations create hypotheses and conclusions that can accumulate and can cause great destruction. Little assumptions about people's character and motives create huge chasms between us that cause our hearts and minds to become hardened and closed to their true situation. Such heart attitudes kill grace.

In order to develop a connection, we need to build bridges. When we look for the best in others, listen, learn, empathize, love, and extend grace, we build relational bridges that can prove to be a lifeline between us. To care for someone, we must let go of the preconceived notions and relinquish our expectations of that person. To care for someone, we must acknowledge his or her present situation and give the gift of grace and acceptance, realizing that what we see is but a very narrow sliver of all that makes up that person. Godly love takes what is presented and seeks to explore and discover more about this person so he or she can be celebrated, not judged. Godly love extends grace.

We have all experienced the hurt of belittling judgments, criticism that lacerates, reproach laced with scorn, unwarranted disapprovals, and personal agendas wrapped in religious rhetoric. We know how painful it is to be on the receiving end of these products of humanity's fall. However, adding the corrective measures of empathy, investigation, and grace will bring about relational change.

Verses to Study

Romans 2:1-4
John 7:24
James 4:11-12
1 Thessalonians 5:11
John 8:1-11
Luke 6:41-42
Romans 13:8-10
Galatians 5:13-15
James 2:1-4
Matthew 12:33-37

Questions for Reflection

1. In what types of situations do you find yourself making quick assumptions and judgments about others? Is there a correlation to either your greatest strengths or your greatest weaknesses?

2. In what situations could you ask more questions and thus make fewer assumptions?

3. What would it look like to be a giver of grace rather than judgment at your workplace?

6 Envy Rejected by Celebration

At one time Stacy loved her job. She had worked hard to go above and beyond her boss's expectations. Despite her creativity and diligence, the scope of work had gone beyond her capabilities. Susan, a new assistant, was hired to work alongside Stacy. In announcing her arrival, the boss went through the usual formalities but then ended his introduction by saying, "Susan, I can't tell you how thrilled I am to have found you and to be bringing you onto this team. Now we'll be able to get things in order and done right! You're such a gifted and talented person—just what this team has been needing."

At first Stacy celebrated the arrival of her new coworker, but the seed of comparison was planted in her heart when she chose to consider the official introductions as a slap against her and an elevation of Susan. *Had her work really been that deficient? Was she considered less than adequate to do the job?* The comparisons that developed in her mind bred a self-righteous anger rooted in jealousy. This feeling of being "less than" only served to distance her from others in the office. Stacy's envy of this new woman kept her from wanting to get to know her.

With every project that Stacy submitted, she worked harder to prove that she was a better and more valuable team member. She became consumed by the need to prove herself.

At her annual evaluation her boss noted that her work had been of the highest quality, but he expressed concern that she had become withdrawn and stressed, which was compromising her ability to be a strong team member. Since this was an esteemed value, Stacy was being placed on probation. She needed to improve her interpersonal skills in order to be a better team player and keep her position.

Stacy had to take stock of her heart. *Was the competition she perceived with Susan a reflection of reality? Did the boss see Susan as being more valuable than Stacy? What if he did? Was it not okay for someone to be better than her? Why was it so important for her to be at the top?* Stacy realized that the issue was not the boss's comparison; the struggle was in her own mind and heart. She had allowed unhealthy comparison to breed the sin of envy. The relational chasm widened.

Do You See the Issue?

Envy and comparisons cause fracture in relationships. We experience the effect of this sin when a coworker is given the promotion we had thought would come our way, and we choose to turn away rather than offer the congratulations he or she deserves. We experience it as we sit in a meeting and listen to a coworker expound on a creative solution that had its beginning in a conversation with us, but he or she accepts all the credit. We experience it when one of our staff announces that she and her husband are going on a cruise, and we quickly recall our own litany of vacations compared to her.

Envy and jealousy run rampant in the hearts and minds of women. We may find ourselves envious of our male coworkers who don't seem to juggle work and home issues, or our friend's quick advancement up the corporate ladder. Envy is not limited to our roles at the workplace. We compare our dress sizes and our paychecks, our husbands and our houses, our spiritual gifts and our accomplishments. Envy can infiltrate any of our relationships, but it has the greatest presence in our relationships with other women. Why is this?

When we see someone as a rival, we view him or her as a threat to our well-being, status, or potential. Our greatest competitors are those who are in equal standing to us but have the potential to somehow overtake us in an area in which we feel particularly vulnerable. An administrative assistant is unlikely to see the CEO as someone with whom to compete—but another administrative assistant is a different story.

Envy and jealousy are sins that go back to the beginning of time. Adam and Eve were tempted when the serpent stirred within them a desire to be free from the limits God had placed on them. The serpent tempted them with the desire to be *like* God. Imagine the thoughts that would go through the mind of the created at being offered the chance to be as good as the Creator. Where there had been only thoughts of gratitude and recognition of lower position, now, based on the serpent's suggestion, there existed the opportunity to close the gap. Our hearts would swell with pride. "Imagine me, a god. That has a nice ring to it. Yes, I can see me making a great god."

In this inaugural sin, comparison that led to envy and pride was planted in the hearts of humanity. Perhaps there's a connection between Eve being the one who succumbed to the serpent's guise and the strength that envy has on the hearts of women. It's most uncommon to find a woman who can honestly say that she does not compare herself in any way to another woman. I know I'm not exempt.

I consider myself a good Christian woman. I go to church. I read my Bible. I follow the Ten Commandments. I'm kind and loving to most people. By all evidence, I don't do too badly at this Christian life, unless you were to read my thoughts. I shudder at the idea of someone capturing and replaying for the whole world the thoughts that run through my mind. Maybe I'm not as good as I thought.

For years I've had an ongoing but very private struggle—at least it was private until now. Wherever I am—a coffee shop, airport, or church pew—I love to watch people. If you were watching me watching people, you would think I was simply observing. But what you wouldn't see is that too often I'm critiquing the people who pass. As painful as this is, let me give you a glimpse into my thoughts to show you just how despicable I can be.

Leaving on a business trip, I feel self-congratulatory about my appearance, my career, and my life as a whole. As I sit in the airport, I place my perspective of myself against the people around me.

I notice Person A:

She seems taller than me, or is it just the stiletto heels that make her legs seem long and willowy? I never could understand how someone could travel in such high heels. They look like expensive Italian leather shoes that probably have a special breathing quality to them. I could probably handle long flights in heels if I had such beautiful leather shoes, if I weighed as little as she weighs, and if I had a business class flying budget. Being that skinny, she probably doesn't have a problem with her feet swelling.

Then along comes Person B wearing sweat pants:

Actually, one couldn't really call them pants; they look more like second-skin polyesters that should have been left at the gym. It doesn't look as if she's been to the gym, though, with that extra weight she's carrying inside those pants.

I no longer feel I need to suck in my stomach. On the contrary, I'm feeling rather elated about my aging figure next to B.

Person C, a man seated next to me, was talking on his cell phone. As the discussion heats up, I'm drawn into this one-sided conversation.

He's very articulate; it's obvious he's a successful business- man. He's very adept at holding to his points. If I was strong and articulate like he is, I wouldn't wimp out on tough conver- sations. I'm pathetic.

Along comes Person D dragging along four little kids under three feet tall:

She looks bedraggled. Why would any sane woman try to get four babies out of bed to catch a seven o'clock A.M. flight? At least I book my family on later flights so we have plenty of time to get to the airport and look like the perfect family. Too bad she can't attend one of my workshops on mothering.

This litany of critiques and comparisons all occur in the span of two minutes. Imagine how many judgments I can make by the end of the day. My thought life is full of comparisons, evaluations, and envy. I'm the poster child for Jesus' condemnation of the Pharisees:

Woe to you, teachers of the law and Pharisees, you hypo- crites! You are like whitewashed tombs, which look beautiful on the outside but on the inside are full of dead men's bones and everything unclean. In the same way, on the outside you appear to people as righteous but on the inside you are full of hypocrisy and wickedness *(Matthew 23:27-28).*

You may be wondering why I use these examples from my own life. What do they have to do with the workplace? The reason is that many of the stories women tell me indicate that much of our envy stems from essentially trivial matters. Statements such as "I real- ized the real reason I didn't like her was because she looked better than me," or "She was smarter than me because she used a certain software, so everyone went to her for help. I just feel dumb." This comparative inner dialogue is affecting our relationships.

As I critique the people around me, I revel in the boost my self-esteem gets by finding someone I deem to be less capable, less beautiful, less articulate, or less put-together than I. Then the pendulum swings, and I find myself beside someone who by comparison has it all together, and I come out with the short end of the stick. The comparison see-saw I choose to ride distances me from God, its self-condemnation rips at my soul, and it broadens the relational chasm.

The Progression of Sin

Consider what James says about the progression of sin:

When tempted, no one should say, "God is tempting me." For God cannot be tempted by evil, nor does he tempt anyone; but each one is tempted when, by his own evil desire, he is dragged away and enticed. Then, after desire has conceived, it gives birth to sin; and sin, when it is full-grown, gives birth to death (*James 1:13-15*).

Envy takes what could otherwise be a benign comparison with another and entices us to want to close the gap. Sin is conceived in our hearts as we refuse to accept the gap. As envy matures, it manifests either by causing us to withdraw—an inability to celebrate others—or we become aggressive, treating others as rivals—the critical spirit. Both destroy relationships.

Where has this leaked into our lives? I daresay it permeates our lives.

We compare our bodies: *I wish my figure was like hers.*

We compare our work situations: *If I was able to go out with the guys after work, then I would have gotten that promotion, and I would be the one sitting in the corner office now.*

We compare our material possessions: *I wish I had the fancy car and big home like the guy down the hallway.*

We compare the men in our lives: *If only my boyfriend would act like my coworker's husband. Now he knows how to treat a woman!*

We compare our spirituality: *I'm much better at displaying humility than she is.*

We compare our worth to God: *If I weren't such a failure, God would love me more, and then He'd find ways to use me like He uses her.*

I believe that our comparison and the envy it breeds grieves the heart of God. Why? Because it's a sin that separates us from God and from others, because envy is a sin. Envy runs rampant, so we must not leave it unchecked if we're to build healthy relationships.

Corrective Measures

There are three things we must do to build a relational bridge where envy has prevailed. The first is to reflect on our thinking, the second is to stop the wrong thinking, and the third is to be filled with an awareness of God's acceptance of us. When we apply these principles, we'll be amazed at the positive effects they can have on our relationships.

The first step is to discern areas in which we're allowing the sin of envy to get a foothold. I believe that envy is conceived when we allow our minds to entertain thoughts of comparison. We may notice differences in people, but at that initial point we come to a fork in the road and must make a split-second decision about where those thoughts are going to take us.

When we see a woman receiving the attention of the men in the workplace because she got her work done quickly and has time to spare while we're still laboring to finish our work, this is the point at which we're faced with a choice. The fork in the road will take us either down the path of celebration or down a path of evaluation that leads to envy.

In order to rid our lives of envy, we must ask God to change us by making us conscious of the thoughts we entertain that are unpleasing to Him. When I asked God to reveal to me the sin in my thoughts, I was shocked to realize how much brain space and minutes in the day were given to comparison. I realized that the only way I was going to stop my thoughts from taking me down the wrong road was to look to God to help me discover the path of love and celebration of others. Before I opened my heart to God's Spirit, I was unable to see where my thoughts were taking me. Then I had to realize my desperate need for God's help to retrain my comparative patterns.

First Corinthians 13, "the love chapter," tells us that love is not envious. When Christ was asked what the greatest commandment was, He responded, "'Love the Lord your God with all your heart and with all your soul and with all your mind.' This is the first and greatest commandment. And the second is like it: 'Love your neighbor as yourself'" (Matthew 22:37-39). In this we are instructed to love God with our minds. If our minds are given over to comparison, that leads to envy, and we're telling Him that what He created is not good enough. Comparison that leads to envy keeps us from loving. No wonder I struggled to love God, myself, and others. I didn't have time in my day to love. Too much of it was consumed with keeping track and comparing myself to others. We're called to pursue "truth in the inner parts" (Psalm 51:6), and God is the disseminator of truth.

If our focus is on God and absorbing His opinion of us, we'll do as the psalmist exhorts: "Direct me in the path of your commands for there I find delight. Turn my heart toward your statutes and not toward self gain. Turn my eyes away from worthless things; preserve my life according to your word" (Psalm 119:35-37). We must let go of all the worthless things we focus on in order to nurture an attitude of contentment and gratitude.

The comparisons I engaged in came from a lack of contentment about who I was and my situation in life. I had rebuffed God's acceptance of me. In order to experience true contentment, I must believe that I'm accepted by God. "God doesn't accept people because they 'measure up,' because they are innocent or strong or admirable. . . . God fully accepts us even though He also fully knows us—our weaknesses, sinfulness and all. He is intimately acquainted with all our ways . . . yet He accepts us now and forever."[1]

"Those the Father has given me will come to me, and I will never reject them" (John 6:37, NLT). Scripture does not say that Jesus died only for those who had their acts together, would be of some value to Him, or are a notch above average. No, it reads, "While we were yet sinners, Christ died for us" (Romans 5:8). God sees value in us, even when we mess up. Nothing we have done, can do, or will do will make God love us less.

It's never a matter of whether or not we're better than someone else. There will always be people who will be faster, smarter, more articulate, thinner, fitter, happier, or richer, to name just a few ways that some outdo others. The issue is not where we rank—it's that we stop the ranking game. We must let go of the drive to come out on top, to be better than the next person. We're admonished to have "godliness with contentment" (1 Timothy 6:6), or as *The Message* puts it, "the rich simplicity of being yourself before God." This is the place where we will find self-acceptance.

The apostle Paul gives testimony to learning contentment:

I've learned by now to be quite content whatever my circumstances. I'm just as happy with little as with much, with much as with little. I've found the recipe for being happy whether full or hungry, hands full or hands empty. Whatever I have, wherever I am, I can make it through anything in the One who makes me who I am *(Philippians 4:11-12, TM)*.

Our contentment must be rooted in our relationship with God. When we're clothed with the Lord Jesus Christ (Romans 13:14), it becomes a moot point to compare our wardrobe to that of the woman in the next cubicle. We'll be content with the wardrobe God has given us, and we'll stop striving to be better than the rest. In fact, we'll be thankful for the clothes we're wearing today as well as what's at home in the closet.

The Esther Connection

Many judgments could be made about Esther. We could say that she was a beauty queen who participated in a pagan ritual of polygamy. We could say that she hid her faith, risking her nation's annihilation. There were a lot of things that Esther seemed to do wrong. But if we follow the example of Christ, we'll see the good in Esther and celebrate it.

Esther came through the agony of losing her parents—not ravaged but stronger. She soaked up the love and teaching of Mordecai. She entered the palace and met the challenge with confidence and humility. She took on the role of queen with poise and integrity. She showed humility in her desire to petition God for protection and blessing. She stood before the king with courage, then bent her knee in submission to his decree. She ruled with fairness and truth. Esther was a woman who lived a life worthy of celebration, not because of how it ended, but because with each step along the way she fulfilled the purpose for which she had been born.

Relationship Results

Comparison can yield healthy results if we use it as an objective benchmark to see areas in our lives that are in need of improvement. It also forms the basis of the concept of modeling, where we learn from watching others ways to improve our behavior and develop character. The problem with comparison comes when it gives way to envy and pride, which either causes us to tear others down to build ourselves up or to beat ourselves up for not being gifted in some area to the same extent as another. The former is characterized as a critical spirit and the latter as an inability to celebrate others.

When we accept the corrective measures of identifying and stopping our thoughts and then embracing with contentment the woman God has made us to be, we'll stop the self-derision and the resulting urgency to be better than others. This will then free us to celebrate others. What has truly amazed me is that when I stay on the relational bridge that celebrates, my thoughts of envy, hatred, or scorn turn into prayer for these women, resulting in growing love and admiration.

How would this play out in my interior conversation as I sat at the airport? Instead of having jealousy toward Person A with the lanky legs and swanky Italian shoes, I would find myself saying, *Thank you, Lord, that you have provided so abundantly for this woman that she has the resources to be comfortable as she flies. Wherever she's going, may she sense your approval of her and bless her endeavors today.*

Instead of scorn for Person B, I would pray, *Lord, help her to feel loved today not just by the people around her, and may she know in the depth of her heart that she's of immeasurable value to you. If she's struggling to lose weight, help her to turn away from foods that are not healthy. Give her strength.*

As I listened to Person C, I would find myself thinking of the people I have in my life from whom I could learn some of the skills this man exhibits, and then instead of envying his abilities, I would listen to see if I could glean something. (Listening in on other's conversations is a whole other topic!)

Finally as I watched Person D and her entourage, I would let go of the feeling of superiority and instead ask that God would give her patience and courage as she traveled with these four small children. I would discover that I was watching her with empathy, wondering if there had been a family tragedy that forced her to travel alone. I can't help but smile when I remember how loving she was with the kids and how well-behaved and courteous they were. Indeed, there's much to celebrate. Notice how praying creates a heart of celebration, and a bridge of care is built toward people I don't even know.

Once God's Spirit has exposed our thoughts, then we can begin to walk a new path in His strength, a path that takes us toward more effectively loving our neighbor and accepting God's love of us. His love added to the equation is the only thing that will stop the cycle of comparison and envy. Trying harder won't work. Self-control will fail. Asking God to help us realize and absorb His love is the only means that will stop envy.

The strengthening or erosion of our relationships starts in our minds and hearts. Think of it this way: Every time we compare ourselves to coworkers and go down the path of envy, we're taking a hammer and weakening or even breaking down our relational bridge. Every time we choose to celebrate who they are and choose to love them, we're building and strengthening the bridge.

Every day when you go to your workplace, be on the lookout for ways you can celebrate. Cheer people on, and congratulate them for the work they're doing. Thank someone for going above and beyond. Look for something positive in all whom you encounter, and sincerely compliment them. Be known as a woman who oozes optimism. Our lives and the lives of our coworkers are worthy of celebration. Each person with whom we interact, each step we take, each job we do, each dream fulfilled becomes a reason to celebrate. Find a reason each day to celebrate someone else, and watch those relational bridges develop.

Let the celebration begin!

Verses to Study

1 Corinthians 13:4

James 1:13-15

Psalm 119:35-37

1 Timothy 6:6-10

Matthew 23:27-28

Philippians 4:11-13

Galatians 5:22-26

Jeremiah 17:9-10

Proverbs 30:12-13

James 3:13-18

Questions for Reflection

1. In what areas do you tend to compare yourself to others—job performance, abilities, possessions, body, relationships?

2. To whom do you feel superior or inferior?

3. Who is the hardest person to pray for? Ask God to reveal if you're entertaining envy toward them.

7 I'm Part of a Team

Workplace relationships require teamwork. If you do your job by yourself, then you need get along with only yourself. But if you work alongside at least one other person, you're part of a team. Although a team is an entity, it's made up of different individuals who each contribute to its success and struggle. Efficient teams don't just happen. For a person to be successful, it's imperative to understand all the members of the team and then discover ways to build and strengthen connections with them based on each one's individuality. Unresolved differences have the potential to erode and tear apart the team. Conversely, recognizing differences and promoting each individual's strengths help enhance the team's production. When each person is able to use his or her strengths, it helps eliminate self-promotion and protectionism and creates a safe environment for a team to flourish. It's within this milieu that healthy workplace relationships can develop.

Patrick Lencioni speaks to this in *The Five Dysfunctions of a Team*: "Not finance. Not strategy. Not technology. It is teamwork that remains the ultimate competitive advantage, both because it is powerful and so rare."[1]

Wired Uniquely

Each of us is wired uniquely. As we work alongside others, it becomes obvious that we approach work from different standpoints, the processes we use to complete tasks vary, and we view accomplishments from own perspectives. Either these distinctions become an obstacle to accomplishing work or they add strength to the mosaic of the workplace.

Imagine that your workplace is a body made up of many parts—some quiet, some expressive, some laid back, some driven—but all necessary. Read these following verses from the perspective that the body being referred to is actually your workplace and the various body parts refer to the types of people who work there:

A body isn't just a single part blown up into something huge. It's all the different-but-similar parts arranged and functioning together. If Foot said, "I'm not elegant like Hand, embellished with rings; I guess I don't belong to this body," would that make it so? If Ear said, "I'm not beautiful like Eye, limpid and expressive; I don't deserve a place on the head," would you want to remove it from the body? If the body was all eye, how could it hear? If all ear, how could it smell? As it is, we see that God has carefully placed each part of the body right where he wanted it. But I also want you to think about how this keeps your significance from getting blown up into self-importance. For no matter how significant you are, it is only because of what you are a part of. An enormous eye or a gigantic hand wouldn't be a body, but a monster. What we have is one body with many parts, each its proper size and in its proper place (*1 Corinthians 12:14-20, TM*).

If we're able to see the value of variety in the workplace, we'll be less likely to try changing people. But that doesn't stop these differences from driving us crazy. So what options do we have in order to get along with others who are not like us?

One option is to continue working in the same rut where we presently find ourselves, characterized by annoyance, stalemate, frustration, and judgment. Predictably, this toxic environment will escalate to the point at which production is hampered, feelings are hurt, and key employees may move on. Or we could choose to build relational bridges by appreciating—even celebrating—the uniqueness each team member brings.

Variety Adds Strength

An important part of accepting other's differences is to see them through the eyes of God, the Creator. He did not make everyone the same. In fact, He made no two people the same. He chose our DNA and then knit us together in our mother's womb (Psalm 139:13) so that we would be wired in a specific way. To try to change someone's natural personality or to ridicule him or her because of the way he or she is wired is to criticize the Designer. Rather, may we be found faithful to celebrate the people around us—even those who are very different than us and who may even threaten to drive us crazy.

Heather was introduced to the study of the personalities in many forms: colors, animals, various combinations of the Myers-Briggs Type Indicator, the DISC descriptors, and other permutations of personality theories. Understanding how critical it was to recognize her own strengths and weaknesses was equally important to the benefit of understanding the personalities of the people around her, especially those on her team. Let's take a peek into the reality of Heather's team, where four of her managers are textbook representatives of the four personality types.[2]

Stanley, the *popular sanguine*, is the loudest and most outgoing person at his workplace. The flurry of excitement he creates is accentuated by his stylish clothing that screams to be noticed. If the job has anything to do with sales, promotion, or interaction with others, he's likely the one who is best for the role. At team meetings Stanley is always full of new and innovative ideas. Unfortunately, he's prone to skipping to the newest opportunity before finishing the routine work of the last.

Martin epitomizes the *perfect melancholy*. He always arrives at work a few minutes early in perfectly pressed pants with a double starched shirt. He's friendly, but in group settings he tends to hang back and observe, as he has no desire to be the center of attention. Martin is known for his detailed analysis and high quality of work. He spends a great deal of time thinking through details and processes before he speaks. His self-expectations are high, and he holds others to this same standard. Martin's desire for perfection is seldom met, so he has to guard against skepticism and criticism creeping into his relationships.

Carol, the *powerful choleric*, is known as the worker, because she's purposeful and focused and accomplishes more than anyone else. Even her clothing is functional: high heels that hinder speed are sidelined for flats, and basic black saves precious time when coordinating outfits. You may be able to detect an air of impatience as she stands with her hands on her hips or her pointer finger wagging in your face as she talks. She usually finds herself in charge of something. She has a knack for noticing what needs to be done and either does it herself or delegates someone else to the job. She can come across as bossy and demanding of others, but her ability to multitask and produce goal-oriented processes wins the loyalty of her coworkers.

Phyllis is the most laid-back person in the department. She saunters into work wearing her casual jeans and a T-shirt whenever she can get away with it. Her phlegmatic motto is "Don't sweat the small stuff," and her tranquility draws people into relationship. She has a natural ability to diffuse tension and mediate solutions. Phyllis is seldom the first person to jump into a project. Rather, she sits back and watches how the team is working and then finds a spot where she feels she can contribute to the team. Making decisions is taxing for Phyllis, but once a decision is made, she stands firmly behind it.

As you were reading about Heather's coworkers, you were probably able to recognize people in your work environment who match many of the characteristics described. It's important to remember that each person we work with is an individual with a unique history, set of values, and challenges. It threatens the team if we make quick judgments that stereotype the members. It takes time to get to know our coworkers. As we do, our view of them will widen and deepen, thereby providing us with a much fuller view of each one's personality type.

This understanding should never be used to judge or criticize. When used constructively, it becomes a helpful tool to understand those around us, allowing us to develop strategies that will strengthen these relationships.

We're now going to eavesdrop on a meeting involving these four personalities to catch a glimpse of how the four individuals interact. As you read, think about how each of them could improve his or her communication with other team members so that relational bridges would be strengthened. Also, be sure to find the parallels to your own relationships.

Together on a Team

A meeting is called, and all four managers are expected to attend. Carol is the first to arrive. Her folders are arranged to match the agenda to avoid wasting any time shuffling papers once the meeting starts. She has figured out the processes that need to occur and thinks this meeting is redundant. Her view is to keep the discussion to a minimum, delegate, and then go at it.

Martin is the next to arrive. He has spent time crunching the numbers and has meticulously prepared his presentation. He takes a deep breath as he enters the room, still rehearsing the details in his mind. Phyllis and Stanley arrive together. Stanley is spinning a yarn about his latest adventure, and Phyllis quietly nods as she takes the seat closest to the door. When the first agenda item is presented, Carol stands up, describes her plan, and charges to the whiteboard to draw out a flow chart. Stanley, who works well with visuals, enters the discussion immediately. His creativity and visioning ability enable him to see outside the box. To Carol, though, these are perceived as curve balls and a threat to her plan. The intensity between Carol and Stanley escalates as both want their ideas understood.

Meanwhile, Martin and Phyllis watch from the sidelines. Finally, out of exasperation Carol turns to Martin and snaps, "Martin, what do you think?" Martin is not prepared for this question. If she had asked him to describe what his numbers indicated, he would have confidently shared his expertise. But to make an unprepared response to this new scenario leaves him feeling tongue-tied. He stammers that he'll need to take some time to think through the best approach. His confidence withers with Carol's exasperation. His assumption is correct that Carol thinks he's inept because he can't think on his feet as well as she can. However, from his vantage point, he's a much more valuable team member because of the precision and thoughtfulness he brings to issues.

Stanley directs a suggestion to Martin, but Martin is running low on patience for Stanley's pie-in-the-sky thinking. By not considering the ramifications of these ideas, Martin questions how anyone can take Stanley seriously. At the same time, Stanley is trying to figure out how someone can be as slow and methodical as Martin. Each is annoyed by the other.

The rising gridlock alerts Stanley to the fact that no one is giving his ideas credence. He decides to change tactics, hoping to get the others to accept his concept. He knows firsthand that encouragement and positive feedback go a long way in getting people on your side. It clicks in his mind that Phyllis has said nothing up to this point, so he invites her contribution. As a peaceful phlegmatic, Phyllis is conciliatory, and because she has been observing, she's able to offer an objective evaluation on how to broker an agreement. This fresh view is grabbed by Carol, who is then able to visualize the next steps. Martin has had a few more minutes to formulate his thoughts and adds a very valuable detail that had previously been overlooked.

As the meeting ends, each member is left with unique thoughts and feelings about what has transpired. The amount of work accomplished is not the most important aspect to Phyllis. Knowing that she was instrumental in ending a deadlock that had threatened the team is much more important to her. It is enough for Stanley to know that his ideas were accepted and have become the initial seed for the end result and that Phyllis and Carol expressed their appreciation for his creative ideas. Carol leaves the meeting with an action plan, but she smugly revels in the notion that, as usual, she has been the driving force. She finds herself thinking, *Can no one else see what needs doing?* Martin leaves with mixed emotions. Carol and Stanley have again stolen the show. Sure, he was able to contribute some key points to be considered, but his hours of preparation and analysis prior to the meeting were somewhat wasted for the sake of speed and conciliation.

Strengthen Through Strengths

This meeting of Stanley, Carol, Martin, and Phyllis was not unlike many others that had previously occurred. Personalities clashed, feelings were hurt, some frustrations were verbalized, and others were swallowed. Much emotional energy went toward judging the other personalities around the table. Each had a celebratory tone about his or her own strengths and the value each brought to the team while focusing on the weaknesses, contributing deficiencies, and annoyances of the others. This pattern of focusing on the weaknesses of others easily becomes a dragnet on a team.

In the bestselling book *Strengths Finder 2.0,* Tom Rath tells of the research conducted by The Gallop Organization that looked at the degree to which employees are engaged or disengaged in their work. "Most surprising is the degree to which having a manager who focuses on our strengths decreases the odds of your being miserable on the job. It appears that the epidemic of active disengagement we see in workplaces every day is a curable disease . . . if we can help the people around us develop their strengths."[3] Helping people realize their strengths and then encouraging them to use those strengths to increase the success of the team will become a win-win situation.

I'm not suggesting that weaknesses be ignored. It's vital to know our weaknesses and how they can develop into blind spots. The benefit of being part of a team is that the team is strongest when one person's weaknesses are covered by another's strengths. Pretending that we're good at everything only puts ourselves and the team at risk. Self-promotion and self-protection erode relationships.

Likewise, when we have a celebratory tone about our own strengths and the value they bring to the team while focusing on the weaknesses and contributing deficiencies and annoyances of the others, our team relationships suffer. This individualistic mind-set is described in these paraphrased words of Jesus: "How do you expect to get anywhere with God when you spend all your time jockeying for position with each other, ranking your rivals and ignoring God?" (John 5:44, TM) To be part of a team that has strong relationships and works effectively, we must put aside our desires to make it to the top alone and rather see ourselves as a team player where we must all arrive at the top together.

We're encouraged to follow the example of Christ, who had equal status with God but willingly set aside the privileges of deity and humbled himself to become a man here on earth who endured death on a cross. Here is how it will look for us. "Don't push your way to the front; don't sweet-talk your way to the top. Put yourself aside, and help others get ahead. Don't be obsessed with getting your own advantage. Forget yourselves long enough to lend a helping hand" (Philippians 2:3-4, TM).

Rather than looking for opportunities to build up ourselves, we should be looking for ways to bring out the strengths of others. This has a huge impact on deepening relationships. Rather than having a self-congratulatory attitude, we should take the time and effort to figure out the personalities of the people we work with and by doing so learn their emotional needs.

Applying the Golden Rule

Society calls it the Golden Rule: "Do to others what you would have them do to you" (Matthew 7:12). Jesus called it "a simple rule of thumb for behavior. Ask yourself what you want people to do for you; then grab the initiative and do it for them!" (Luke 6:31, TM). This is the secret of relationship success. Florence Littauer applies the Golden Rule to the importance of understanding the personalities of others. "With all the various personalities we encounter every day, we need skills and help to give them what they want. Because all people have different needs and desires according to their personalities, we have to learn how to meet these needs."[4]

Without being cognizant of it, we interact with others through our own personalities. When that interaction is with someone who has a personality different from ours, it's as if we're speaking a language that he or she does not understand. Let's say these four managers we just mentioned speak Chinese, Spanish, Finnish, and Swahili. It would not matter if they talked more loudly, more slowly, or even spelled out the words—if the other person doesn't understand the language, communication is flawed. We must learn to communicate in such a way that it meets the emotional needs of the other person.

This can occur through little courtesies that go a long way toward building sturdy relational bridges. Knowing that Martin prefers to formulate his thoughts before speaking, Carol could have posed her question as "I value everyone's input and would like to know what each of you thinks." This would reduce the stress placed on one person to speak immediately and provide Martin with the time to prepare the "perfect" delivery essential for a melancholy. Rather than dismissing Stanley's creative ideas as pie-in-the-sky, Martin could have chosen to see how valuable these ideas were to the team's process—even if they were very different from how he would have approached it. For Carol, she would have felt valued if someone had patted her on the back and acknowledged her strong work and keen eye for business solutions. It bolstered Phyllis to know that she was appreciated and that her input had been useful.

Often in situations like this team meeting, a self-congratulatory attitude keeps us from taking the time and effort to figure out the personalities of the people we work with and understanding their emotional needs. By choosing to interact with them in ways that meet their emotional needs, we'll build bridges with them rather than deepen the chasm.

Letting go of the expectation that everyone should be like us is an important step to building relational bridges. Seeing the good in others and learning their emotional needs will strengthen those connections. Finally, looking at the best way to treat others to foster their sense of self-worth helps us build an environment in which kinship develops. These are foundational toward designing, building, and maintaining relationships.

The Esther Connection

Esther spent her life around people with whom she developed strong relationships and the ability to work together. With God's help, Esther was able to interact with people in such a way that drew them into a close relationship of trust and allegiance. Upon entering the palace with the other virgins from the land, Esther was taken under the tutelage of Hegai, the eunuch in charge of the king's harem. There was something about Esther's character that drew Hegai and others to her and granted her favor with them. This was repeated with King Xerxes as she won his favor and approval. Esther was cognizant of her need to stay connected to Mordecai, even though he was outside the palace and she was inside. When it came time to pray for God's blessings, she beseeched Mordecai to get the Jewish community to join her and her maidens in a fast. Esther is a strong example of someone who could have decided to go it alone but instead embraced the strength that came with being part of a team.

There is no indication that Esther had studied how to use the knowledge of personalities to build relational bridges, but by virtue of how she was able to get along with others, she must have been attuned to the emotional needs of those around her. She was attentive to when there was a change in Mordecai's behavior and took seriously his representation of grief, knowing he was not simply seeking attention. She also was able to discern, through God's help, that Haman was full of self-importance. By accentuating his pride, she could draw him in and make him vulnerable. Inviting him not just once, but twice, to a banquet played into this aspect of his personality. Esther's knowledge of Xerxes would have helped her understand his strengths and weaknesses. Her display of courage and her enchanting but decisive behavior intrigued him so much that he offered her anything—even half his kingdom.

Esther did not use her ability to get along with others for her own selfish purposes. Rather, God bestowed on her the ability to build relational bridges so that His purposes would unfold.

Verses to Study

Galatians 6:3-5
2 Corinthians 13:5
Philippians 3:12-16
Matthew 7:1-5
1 Corinthians 12:12-27
John 5:44
Luke 6:31
Romans 12:18
Philippians 1:6

Questions for Reflection

1. List all the strengths and weaknesses you can think of that you bring to your job. Do the same for the people with whom you work closely. Take a look at ways they complement each other to strengthen the team.

2. Is there a particular coworker you struggle to get along with? What parts of his or her personality irritate you? What heart change do you need to experience in order to show that person greater love?

3. What would it look like for you to apply the Golden Rule to your workplace relationships?

8 I'm the Boss

Every day Monica goes to work contemplating both the privilege and responsibility of her role. She had experienced the truth of Robert Frost's words "By faithfully working eight hours a day, you may eventually get to be a boss and work twelve hours a day."[1] She has sacrificed holidays to address a critical development that threatened production. She missed her daughter's school drama because she was out of town at the annual team-building event. She has anguished over the loss of a friendship when she was promoted and became her friend's leader rather than her peer. She has some regrets, but for the most part she loves her job, thrives in her role as leader, and savors the privilege to pour herself into the lives of her staff.

Often, though, as she drives home at the end of a long day, she feels like an island. She's surrounded by people at work, but because she's the boss, she's separated from them. She's a part of the team, but her role places her in a unique position. She's at risk of becoming isolated, aloof, and disconnected if she consciously builds bridges between herself and her employees. In her supervisory role, she has a fiduciary position to ensure the company mandate is achieved, but she's not a slave-driver. She has taken enough leadership training to reinforce the value she holds deep in her soul that the most important commodity at any workplace is the people.

To live out this value, Monica consistently makes many small but significant choices to build relational bridges with those people who report to her. Each bridge between her and an employee is unique, yet the similarities are based on guiding principles that steer her actions.

There's no shortage of books and articles written to expand our knowledge and to speak into our experiences as leaders, and I'll draw on the wisdom of experts. In order to be true to my initial premise, I'm deferring our greatest example on leadership to what Scripture tells us about Jesus. His leadership character and the way He treated people are the two guiding principles we will apply to our own situations as supervisors and leaders. We may be at the helm of a thousand-person company, or we may give leadership to two. Regardless, we must contemplate our character and our actions, including the effect they have on building a strong relational bridge.

Humility

Our leadership idea may be based on the belief that we must be strong and confident. Any crack in that facade puts us at risk of being viewed as wishy-washy and not worthy of our employees' respect.

Society portrays mighty leaders as being outspoken stateswomen such as Margaret Thatcher, social engineers such as Oprah Winfrey, or bold decision-makers such as Carly Fiorina, former CEO of Hewlett-Packard. All these women portray strong leadership qualities; but these are not the only examples we could emulate.

Jesus Christ, the Son of God, the Creator of all things—including the concept of leadership—demonstrated what it means to be a leader who leads from a heart of humility rather than an attitude of greatness.

Think of yourselves the way Christ Jesus thought of himself. He had equal status with God but didn't think so much of himself that he had to cling to the advantages of that status no matter what. Not at all. When the time came, he set aside the privileges of deity and took on the status of a slave, became human! Having become human, he stayed human. It was an incredibly humbling process. He didn't claim special privileges. Instead, he lived a selfless, obedient life and then died a selfless, obedient death—and the worst kind of death at that—a crucifixion (*Philippians 2:5-8, TM*).

It's easy enough to say that we need to be humble like Christ, but how do we foster an attitude of humility in the reality of our workplace?

In Jim Collins' book *Good to Great,* he set out to discover the factors that moved companies from being simply good to being really great. One of the most poignant findings was his description of what he calls a "Level Five Leader." Here he describes a leader as someone who "builds enduring greatness through a paradoxical blend of personal humility and professional will."[2]

He goes on to say "good-to-great leaders didn't talk about themselves," and those who worked with them used words like "quiet, humble, modest, reserved, shy, gracious, mild-mannered, self-effacing, understated, did not believe in his own clippings."[3] Are these not similar adjectives used to describe Jesus?

When we allow God supremacy in our hearts and lives, His humble character will replace our need to protect, promote, or prove ourselves. God-centered humility will produce a much stronger leader than simply outspokenness, social engineering, or bold decisions.

Holly had been handed the leadership of a multi-million-dollar project to create and produce a Broadway-type musical within her city. Her strong project management skills, as well as her love of the arts, were the deciding factors in her being chosen to lead this project. She set about identifying the specialist functions that were needed to contribute to the team. When she approached each person, she cast a vision, not just for the magnitude of the production but also for the significant role each could contribute. It didn't take long for Holly to recruit a team who could efficiently create this production.

When the curtain closed on opening night, Holly stood beside the chairman of the arts board as he fielded questions from the media about the success of this production. "How do you feel about tonight's production, sir?" The chairman stepped up to the microphone and said, "I'm thrilled that we've been able to bring a production of this quality to our city. I knew we had talent in this city, and I'm so glad to have found it. This is just the beginning of a resurgence of art. You'll be hearing more from me."

The reporter then turned to Holly and asked, "As the producer of this show, to what do you attribute its success?" Holly had cringed at the self-congratulatory comments of the chairman, so as she stepped up to speak, she asked God to give her words of humility.

"This production is in no way my doing alone," she said, "from each cast member to Anne, our choreographer; Charles, our props manager; Marianne, on costumes; and a huge crew of technical and support staff. We had 127 community volunteers who came to usher, hand out programs, and serve coffee at the break, and many will be here late into the night cleaning up. I could go on and on. The success of this project rests on the shoulders of each person who contributed in some big or small way. The accolades go to them."

Rather than grabbing the spotlight and enthusiastically accepting the praise that rightfully came her way, Holly attributed the success to others. Humility destroys independence. Pride, the antithesis of humility, causes us to believe we're self-sufficient and need others only to the degree that they serve our accomplishments. Humility recognizes our need for God and others.

Jim Collins would say that this is an example of Level Five Leadership: "Level Five leaders look out the window to apportion credit to factors outside themselves when things go well (and if they cannot find a specific person or event to give credit to, they credit good luck)."[4] All too often we emulate the chairman in this story, who chose to "preen in front of the mirror and credit [himself] when things went well."[5]

Humility is a very narrow road for leaders. Following the narrow path of humility that Christ modeled may not be the easiest way to build relational bridges with the people who look to you for leadership, but the trust that it produces will withstand many more torrents than a bridge built on showmanship, self-centeredness, and substandard materials.

Take Personal Responsibility

As important as it is to deflect praise away from ourselves, it's equally important to take responsibility for our actions and not look for someone else to blame when things are less than great. This requires knowing your strengths and weaknesses. As the apostle

Paul wrote, "Don't think you are better than you really are. Be honest in your evaluation of yourselves, measuring yourselves by the faith God has given us" (Romans 12:3, NLT). As humble leaders, we must be committed to developing and widening our skill-base and leadership abilities. Our human limitations will keep us from being good at everything.

The stereotypical male-female designation is that men are logical and higher functioning in their left-brain capabilities, while women excel in areas that require right-brain dominance. While God created each woman as unique, our femininity may cause us to be more naturally competent in our right-brain functioning. The fact that we're in positions of leadership will give evidence, though, that we've also developed strength with our left-brain function. To be great leaders, we must become life-long learners, both about ourselves and about those around us. Developing our abilities to utilize both sides of our brains will help us develop stronger leadership skills and build healthy connections to those we lead.

Author Steven Covey makes the following statement about the need to lead from a perspective that utilizes the strengths of both sides of our brain:

> People who are excellent managers but poor leaders may be extremely well-organized and run a tight ship with superior systems and procedures and detailed job descriptions. But unless they are internally motivated, little gets done because there is no feeling, no heart; everything is too mechanical, too formal, too tight, too productive. . . . A strategic leader can provide direction and vision, motivate through love, and build a complementary team based on mutual respect if he or she is more effectiveness-minded than efficiency-minded, more concerned with direction and result than with methods, systems, and procedures.[6]

As women leaders, we have the opportunity to profoundly affect the people who look to us for both management and leadership. To use Stephen Covey's words again, the best boss will be someone who "manages from the left and leads from the right."[7]

Unwavering Resolve

Jesus knew why He had come to earth—He was here to do the will of His Father. His focused determination meant that He was able to give His followers what they needed in order to commit to His purpose. He was a strong leader who communicated to His followers their roles; He was able to cast a larger vision of who they could be; He was able to reward them according to their needs, and He cared for them as individuals. Christ's example of how the perfect leader interacted with His followers will become our textbook for learning how to build strong bridges with our employees.

As leaders in the workplace, we recognize that our responsibility is first to the owners. We're given the task of doing the best we can to steward the organization's resources towards its goals. Our purpose is to see what needs to be done and then have the unwavering resolve to do all that we can to make it happen. One way this plays out is to ensure that we communicate the vision and our expectations to our employees. By establishing and communicating deliverables, our employees will know what's expected of them. This clarity will develop trust in leadership and create healthy reciprocal communication regarding goals.

Kristin remembers reporting to a boss who did not clearly communicate his expectations. His subordinates were confused as to the target they were to hit, and it felt as if they were throwing darts in the dark, hoping to come close to getting it right. Kristin often left a meeting thinking, *Am I the only dummy here? I feel like I don't know what we're doing.*

Now that Kristin is in a leadership role, she tries very hard to be clear with her staff. When the economic downturn shredded the company's bottom line, Kristin gave her employees the heads-up that if sales numbers did not improve, the company would be facing a fifteen-percent staff reduction. By being up-front with them, Kristin was able to generate trust and provide them with some sense of control over doing what they could to turn things around. If she had not been honest with them, the rumor mill would have burned up a great deal of time and left staff guessing if anything would have an impact on a sinking ship. If layoffs came as a surprise, the critical staff who remained would have a lower level of trust for leadership who had kept them in the dark.

Kristin soon discovered that if her employees knew that she was honest, fair, and would do all she could for them, their loyalty would be reciprocated. King Solomon wrote these words to describe a king who was worthy of being followed: "He will deliver the needy who cry out, the afflicted who have no one to help. He will take pity on the weak and the needy and save the needy from death. He will rescue them from oppression and violence, for precious is their blood in his sight. Long may he live!" (Psalm 72:12-15). These wise words about leadership apply equally to female leaders. Having professional will and personal fortitude to do whatever is needed to manage well makes us good stewards of the organization's resources, including its people. That's material for a strong relational bridge from leader to staff in the workplace.

Cast a Larger Vision

Is it not true that each one of us could be better than we are? Developing a vision for what people can be—not just for what they are today—should spur us to do all we can to help them reach their potential. Management consultant Lisa Haneberg compares the role of managers in helping bring people back on course and getting them where they need to be to a Global Positioning System (GPS): "I like how the GPS uses the same pleasant tone no matter how many times we veer off course. Managers would be well-served to learn from this. Recalculating the route is a normal daily management task, and should not be a source of irritation or frustration. It is why we are here and why we are needed.[8]

Helping to direct and redirect our employees toward the attainment of greater horizons is a privilege.

Christ spoke a vision over Peter before leaving for heaven. Peter's abysmal denials of Christ did not stop Jesus from envisioning his becoming the rock on which the Church would be built (Matthew 16:18). As Larry Crabb writes, "We accept people for who they are, we grieve every failure to live out their true identity, and no matter what happens, we continue to believe in what they could become without demanding that it happen on our timetable or for our sakes, or that we play a big part in making it happen. Everyone is a work in progress."[9]

Having a vision for people comes from the core belief that God has started something good in each of us and that He is going to continue to work in us until it is completed (Philippians 1:6). Again, everyone is a work in progress, and as leaders we have the opportunity to come alongside and feed that vision.

Elizabeth had been the recipient of this kind of vision-casting. She had come into this company at an entry-level job with a bachelor's degree in business. She had a few years of experience with another firm but landed in this company feeling rather inadequate for the challenge it presented. Her boss at that time gave her a project that stretched her in one particular area, but with the help of his encouragement and guidance, its successful completion led to bigger projects with greater responsibilities.

Elizabeth had worked in this position only a couple of years when her boss came into her office, closed the door, and sat down in the chair. Her immediate fears were quickly allayed as he proceeded to cast a vision of her abilities stretching beyond her job.

She anticipated the word "promotion" coming next, but what she heard was "return to school." The boss saw that her abilities superseded what was being demanded of her in her current position. He was encouraging her go to back to college to further her education. Along with that suggestion were very practical ways the company would support her.

No one had ever suggested that Elizabeth was MBA material, but as she contemplated it, she realized the synergy between her God-given abilities and her heart's desire. She prayed for and received peace in her spirit that confirmed that this was not just her boss's idea or a longing of heart, but it was the direction God was leading her. She followed up on her boss's suggestion and returned to school.

Upon her graduation, it seemed too good to be true that the company had a position waiting for her. But it got even better when the CEO came to compliment her accomplishments and suggested ways she could continue to hone her skills. His encouraging affirmation, along with the resources he made available, gave her the courage and the skills to become all that God had created her to be. Throughout her career she was esteemed as an expert in her company and in the industry.

Reflecting with thankfulness on the influence her boss had on her, Elizabeth says, "I'll never cease to be grateful that he believed in me, sometimes stretched me beyond my limit. But because he had confidence in me, I did my best to not disappoint him."

Having personally experienced the impact of a leader's vision, Elizabeth is now committed to being watchful and discerning of potential in others. She uses her role as a leader to cast that vision and help them become more than they may presently believe is possible.

Tangible and Intangible Rewards

In the economic boom that began in the late years of the twentieth century, a higher salary was not always the highest priority of new hires, particularly those just entering the workforce. Rather than more money, prospective employees wanted greater job flexibility, perks that included lifestyle improvements, and more vacation. They saw salary as simply a means of supporting their lifestyles. Given this reality and budgetary squeezes, the effective employer ascertained that he or she had to be creative in finding both tangible and intangible ways to reward his or her employees.

Extending the Golden Rule becomes a significant option for a boss desiring to recognize an employee's hard work. We can wrongly make the assumption that whatever we think is important will be esteemed important by others. Likewise, if we make the assumption that our employees know that we think they're doing a commendable job but we never verbally recognize or praise them for a job well done, we've lost an opportunity to build and strengthen the relational bridge.

A *sanguine* employee needs to feel affirmed, so being praised in a variety of ways will always be well received. Highlighting the ingenuity of the sanguine employee in a team meeting and then allowing him or her to share with the group the humorous things that happened during the span of a project communicates that he or she is a valuable and highly regarded member of the team.

A *melancholy* employee needs to feel understood. Asking if there's anything he or she needs to do the job better will communicate that you care about the quality of work being produced, that you're very aware of the employee's diligence, and you wish to reward him or her by facilitating that "perfectly" completed job.

A *choleric* employee will feel rewarded when he or she has accomplished the task and appreciation is expressed for his or her hard work.

Encouragement of the person's character and its positive effect on his or her accomplishments energizes a *phlegmatic* worker.

A man finds joy in giving an apt reply—and how good is a timely word! *(Proverbs 15:23)*.

Having an eye for specific individual accomplishments and expressing gratitude can repair and cement even the most fragile relationships.

It's our tendency to withhold the intangible rewards until the job is finished. We fear that if we hand out praise too soon, the employee will feel free to slack off and start winding down. But the truth is that affirmation, understanding, appreciation, and encouragement given at critical times during the project may be the most important reward you can give, because it's these intangible rewards that spur people on.

Another way our words can be a gift, albeit with more care than usual, is the willingness to embark on tough conversations. Ignoring a situation to avoid conflict does no one any favors. Suzanne recounts that when she recognized that a difficult conversation needed to take place, notwithstanding its discomfort, she dared not ignore it and hope the situation would go away. Rather, she spent the time necessary working through the best way to address the issue, praying for God's wisdom and direction. "The tongue of the wise brings healing" (Proverbs 12:18).

It's with the voice of experience of someone who by nature would shy away from potential conflict that Suzanne could say, "My employees are always appreciative of a leader who first addresses difficult situations and secondly does so in a dignified manner."

Carefully chosen words that reflect reality are the greatest reward you can give your employees. They cost you nothing, but the dividends of respect, improved focus, and increased motivation are rewards that are good for everyone.

Care for the Whole Individual

Caring for others is important on a number of levels. At its most basic, people who are cared about return that care to others. People who are shown care work more effectively with and for the people who show that care. Cared-for people feel better and are more positive to be around and work with than people who are ignored. Caring about others doesn't have to be a soft or counselor activity—it simply means trying to show reasonable concern for direct reports in every way possible to help them perform and grow.[10]

Karyn was sitting in her office scouring the final draft of the year-end report due to be submitted to her boss the next day. She heard someone pass in the hall but controlled the urge to look up. A few paragraphs later she recognized the sound of the heels that just passed and were now clicking closer to her door and stopping. Again she refrained from looking up in hopes the person would just keep going if she saw how engrossed Karyn was in her work. The gentle knock on the door required a response.

Karyn looked up to see Cindy standing at the door. "I know you're busy, but can I talk to you for a minute?" Cindy asked tentatively.

Pushing aside the report so she wouldn't be tempted to multitask, Karyn invited Cindy to sit down and share what was on her mind. As the story unfolded, Karyn's heart went out to Cindy.

Things were tough at home for Cindy. Her son had been arrested for shoplifting, her daughter was withdrawn and angry, her mother was developing Alzheimer's, and the tension with her husband was mounting daily. In the midst of this she felt completely overwhelmed. Despite considerable sleep, the fatigue would not abate. As Cindy spoke, tears welled up in her eyes and spilled down her cheeks. She apologized that she couldn't seem to keep it all together and admitted that she felt as though she was sinking at both work and home.

As Karyn listened, a question that she knew came from the Holy Spirit flooded her heart and mind. *How can I love God by loving Cindy?* Just as Karyn had pushed aside the project to listen to Cindy, so, too, she had to push aside the impulse to "project manage," with a quick fix or to simply pick up the phone and refer her case to Human Resources. Karyn was alert to the fact that she could easily take on an attitude of judgment that would label why Cindy's life was so messed up, especially compared to her own. Instead, by displaying empathy, she was moved to connect with Cindy.

Karyn had before her an opportunity to reach out to a fellow human being and show that she cared. Her simple question to Cindy, "How can I help?" moved her from lofty supervisor who had only the company's productivity interests at heart to a caring person who wanted to be a conduit of God's love to this hurting woman.

The workplace is too often a reflection of an independent society where asking for help is seen as a weakness. Persons in leadership roles have the opportunity to create a different milieu. By offering to personally help versus pulling out the company policy, we break down the walls of independence and allow God's love to pour in. We gain the privilege of being a part of the miracle of God "healing the broken hearted and binding up their wounds" (Psalm 147:3). What an incredible opportunity to show care and concern for more than just the work employees do but also for who they are as whole persons!

Leadership comes with privilege and responsibility. If we don't enter into this role with humility and a fierce determination to do all that we can to make the company great, we may see our lofty position only as an opportunity for personal gain.

You can climb too high for your own good. It's possible to ascend too far, stand too tall and elevate too much.

Linger too high at high altitudes, and two of your senses suffer. Your hearing dulls. It's hard to hear people when you are higher than they. Voices grow distant. Sentences seem muffled. And when you are up there, your eyesight dims. It's hard to focus on people when you are so far above them. They appear so small. Little figures with no faces. You can hardly distinguish one from the other. They all look alike.

You don't hear them. You don't see them. You are above them.[11]

If you're a boss, if you expand your view of why you go to work, you'll use your skills to accomplish tasks but will also realize that you're more than a taskmaster. You'll make a difference by caring for people but will be more than a caregiver. You've been placed by God where you are for a reason. You're with this company, with these people, for such a time as this. And day after day you'll see evidence of this. Your place is to love God by doing your best for your company as unto the Lord and to love the people around you. By proving to your staff that you're trustworthy, by helping them cast a vision of all they can become, by giving them what they need in order to maximize their accomplishments, by rewarding their efforts, and by offering love and care, you'll be following Jesus' example of leadership—one that's worthy to be followed.

Leadership is a high calling, and being the boss is not easy. In the pursuit to become a leader like Christ, take comfort in these words from 2 Peter 1:3—"His divine power has given us everything we need for life and godliness through our knowledge of him who called us by his own glory and goodness." With God's help you can become a boss who designs, builds, and maintains strong relational bridges.

The Esther Connection

Esther came into the king's palace as a nobody. Even her ancestral heritage went unobserved. At the time, it must have seemed surreal for this young Jewish woman to find herself in the inner palace at Susa. The scriptural account tells us that Esther met the challenge with dignity and integrity. She rose to the position God had prepared her for as Queen of Persia.

However, Esther soon found herself with a much more daunting task than any she had previously faced. She had been given the responsibility, by virtue of her privileged role, to make a difference for others. She carried the weight of her entire nation on her shoulders. Esther placed personal preservation as secondary to that of standing up and protecting others. Certainly she enjoyed the perks that came with her position, but she was willing to forfeit that for a much greater cause—the opportunity to make a difference in the lives of many others. Esther met the challenge of her role and is remembered today as a truly courageous leader.

Verses to Study

Philippians 2:5-8
Romans 12:3-8
Matthew 16:17-19
Proverbs 12:18

Psalm 147:3
2 Peter 1:3-9
Philippians 1:6
Isaiah 50:4

Questions for Reflection

1. In what way do you struggle with remaining humble in your supervisory role?

2. Is there someone with whom you work closely you could influence and encourage to a broader vision? What could you do to help that person reach his or her greater potential?

3. After reading this chapter, how do you sense God is calling you to be a boss who is more like Jesus?

9 I'm *Not* the Boss

Browsing through the local bookstore provided a treasure for Michelle. Her spirit felt buoyed by the fact that she had finally found a book that spoke to her situation and from which she could glean some understanding on how to interact with her immediate supervisor. With her latest purchase secured in a paper bag and tucked under her arm, she could hardly wait to get on the Metro to start to read. Oblivious to those around her who came and went at each stop, Michelle devoured the material in her new book. She was unaware of the person who sat down beside her until the familiar voice greeted her.

"Hi. Fancy meeting you on this train." It was her boss.

As Michelle looked up with a nervous smile, her mind raced as to how to inconspicuously hide her reading material. Before she could slip it back into its brown paper enclave, Michelle's boss asked the fateful question: "What are you reading?"

Michelle felt like the kid caught with her hand in the cookie jar. As she turned the book over, its title screamed *When Smart People Work with Dumb Bosses*.

This nightmarish scenario sends us into a cold sweat as we recall certain bosses we've worked for over the years. Some were competent; others were slackers. Some were encouraging; others cut us to the quick. Some proved to be dream bosses; others gave Godzilla competition.

If we've had the privilege of working for someone who showed integrity and whom we could respect and trust, we know that it's easy to build relational bridges to strong leaders, because they're contributors to the relational bridges that span the chasm between us. They look out for our best interests and are free with encouragement and support. These relationships are rich and play a significant role in the development of our skills and job satisfaction. The opportunity to work under their tutelage reaps great rewards. Being mentored by such a boss is a privilege. In order to glean as much as possible from him or her, we must have a heart that's open to learn, a mind that's attentive, and a spirit that's receptive to correction. Great potential awaits such positive and healthy relationships.

However, such positive scenarios are not always reality. What if our boss is difficult, uncaring, and demanding? What if he or she is a leader who does not warrant being followed? What if our boss has little interest in building healthy relational bridges? As a subordinate, what are we called to? How can we be employees who follow God's principles?

Each of us who has a person above us on the organizational chart needs to do a regular check-up to assess our state of heart. Scripture tells us to "Keep vigilant watch over your heart; that's where life starts" (Proverbs 4:23, TM). When our attitude slips, we need to be vigilant to check those little fires of discontent and disrespect that can cause erosion in our hearts and result in our relationship with our boss being less than it could be. Let's take a look at what must happen in an employee's heart so that a strong relational bridge can be built with the boss.

A Biblical Directive

Imagine that what follows here is a code of ethics posted on your workplace door, and before you enter you must sign in by placing your right hand on the Holy Bible and promising to meet these expectations to the best of your ability. Could you sign off on the following?

- Do what your boss tells you to do.
- Do your best, not just the minimum of what will get you by.
- Be a cheerful worker. A sullen worker will produce shoddy work.
- Assume responsibility for your actions and attitudes.
- Work from your heart.
- Remember—you're not the boss around here.
- Keep in mind who your real Boss is.

This code of ethics comes right out of the Bible:

Servants, do what you're told by your earthly masters. And don't just do the minimum that will get you by. Do your best. Work from the heart for your real Master, for God, confident that you'll get paid in full when you come into your inheritance. Keep in mind always that the ultimate Master you're serving is Christ. The sullen servant who does shoddy work will be held responsible. Being a follower of Jesus doesn't cover up bad work (*Colossians 3:22-25, TM*).

Good for Us

Having a supervisor to whom we're accountable can actually be good for us. Learning to submit to authority is something we start to develop as an infant and must continue throughout life. Submission to authority can be much more difficult for some people than others. Those of us who are independent, visionary, and have a take-charge, choleric personality will naturally find it harder to work at someone else's direction. This gets even more difficult when pride, arrogance, and a stubborn spirit enter the picture. I speak from experience on this.

I once had a friend comment that she would not want to be my supervisor. I was surprised by her statement, but as I thought about it, I realized that what she was really commenting on was that she saw a headstrong streak in me that resisted submission to authority. I realized that her statement was a true reflection of my heart's resistance to God's leading. Can you relate? Each of us must learn to be a better employee—or, as Scripture puts it, a "servant" who works in the service of another.

Obedience

As children we were expected to obey our teachers and parents. Now that we're adults, certainly we can set our own course rather than having to do as we are told. Right? Imagine what would happen when we were behind the wheel of a car if we took the stance that we did not have to obey the laws of the road. Every driver could do what he or she pleased; self-preservation and self-satisfaction would take precedence over the greater good.

Is it any different in the workplace? God has ordained governing authorities and has instructed us to submit ourselves to authority. "There is no authority except that which God has established. The authorities that exist have been established by God" (Romans 13:1).

The boss has been placed in a position of authority, and employees have been put in place to serve him or her. We must have a servant heart so that we can willfully carry out the boss's instructions. Resistance to the boss's direction may very well indicate a heart that lacks humility. We're admonished to think more highly of others than of ourselves and to put the interests of others ahead of our own. This is what Christ exemplified when He was obedient to the point of death—even death on a cross (Philippians 2:3-8).

Obedience in a situation that you are agreeable to and that aligns with your convictions is much easier than finding yourself fighting the thought *This is the most stupid idea my boss has ever come up with. Why am I wasting my time?*

There will always be different vantage points and different ways of tackling projects. Following God's call to be a servant means that you swallow your pride and do the job as outlined. You may be in a position to add your perspective to strengthen the outcome, but if not, you're simply to follow orders, assuming they're legal, moral, and ethical.

One hindrance to obedience is a lack of definition of role and responsibilities. What does your boss expect you to do? What are you authorized to do? What is out of bounds?[1]

If your answers to these questions are vague, you may be hard-pressed to obey your boss's directives. Clear delineation of roles will make it possible to attain desired outcomes, averting mayhem. But don't assume that clear roles and responsibilities are solely the supervisor's job. Raise the matter yourself if things seem unclear.

It's entirely possible that at some time in your career you'll be placed in a situation in which you're asked to compromise your values. Requests or even demands that are immoral or illegal may be placed upon you. If you find yourself in that predicament, you can be certain that these fall outside your responsibility to be obedient. Our Scripture-based values, our company policies and procedures, and the laws and regulations of the land will usurp a workplace leader who is asking us to do something that's not in compliance with these rules.

You should first seek certainty from your boss that you understand what's being asked of you. If it remains a problem, you'll need to take it to a higher level in the organization or simply resign. A key verse to live by is "Whatever happens, conduct yourselves in a manner worthy of the gospel of Christ" (Philippians 1:27).

Tammy led a team who had worked hard on a project of wide scope for the company. To reward her team, her boss invited them to a celebratory luncheon. When the bill arrived, Tammy's boss slipped it to her and said, "You pick this one up. My expense account is already pretty full, but I'll make sure it gets through." Tammy knew that what she had been asked to do was against company policy. The person with the highest signing authority was always supposed to take the bill. Tammy's boss had placed her in an uncomfortable situation by asking her to do something that would make him look good but could end up being a black mark on her record.

Situations like this are common. Covering up for the boss when it's illegal or immoral is never acceptable, and although the choice may be clear, it's never easy. At the other end of the spectrum, we must set aside our own agendas so that we can follow God's plan and willfully obey the boss.

You may wonder how your boss got to be in the position he or she is in, and you may feel you could do a better job if you were in that position. Ineptitude is a reality. Simply because someone holds a position does not mean that the person has acquired the skills necessary to be in that position. Two things to remember are that at some point you may find yourself in a similar situation, and you'll be seeking grace. Doing all that you can to help the boss succeed will mean standing in the gap for his or her inadequacies.

Second, if we trust that God is the final judge, we will be less concerned about making things fair. This is how Jesus dealt with being taken advantage of: "When they hurled their insults at him, he did not retaliate; when he suffered, he made no threats. Instead, he entrusted himself to him who judges justly" (1 Peter 2:23). *The Message* puts it this way: "He suffered in silence, content to let God set things right."

Give It All You Have

"This is your lot in life and in your toilsome labor under the sun. Whatever your hand finds to do, do it with all your might" (Ecclesiastes 9:9-10). Once we've decided that we'll obey the instruction received, we then have a choice to make that will affect how well we do the work. We can begrudgingly obey and give a nod to obedience by doing just the bare minimum, or we can give it all we have and go above and beyond the boss's expectations for the job. That's what we're encouraged to do in these two New Testament passages that talk about boss-servant relationships:

Don't just do what you have to do to get by, but work heartily, as Christ's servants doing what God wants you to do. And work with a smile on your face *(Ephesians 6:6, TM)*.

Whatever you do, work at it with all your heart, as working for the Lord, not for men *(Colossians 3:23)*.

Obedience to a supervisor while harboring passive aggression or outright hostility is not meeting God's criteria. Choosing to go above and beyond simply for selfish reasons, such as to be noticed or to receive accolades, is not an attitude that pleases God. What happens in the heart is always more important than actions.

Respect and Honor

You may choose to obey your boss through your outward actions, and you may even decide to work heartily for him or her, but respecting and honoring your boss takes this farther into a heart issue. This is easy to do if you have a boss who treats you with respect, shows consideration, and truly cares about you. But how do you treat a boss who is demanding, unreasonable, and uncaring? How do you build relational bridges with someone who does not appear to deserve your respect?

"Ask yourself what you want people to do for you, then grab the initiative and do it for *them*" (Matthew 7:12, TM). I'm sorry I couldn't find a way to soften this verse. I know it would have felt better to stroke your bruised ego by saying that you can get even with your boss or, in an underhanded manner, do him or her in. But Christ didn't give us that option. He didn't give us any wiggle room on this topic. We're to treat the boss—no matter how good or bad, worthy or unworthy—with respect and honor. If our hearts are right on this point, our actions will follow. We'll speak to the boss with courteous regard. We'll avoid being pulled into the chatter that complains and backstabs.

The Great Reversal

As an executive assistant, Marci was pleased to be moving up the ladder with her boss when he was granted a huge promotion. As a result, her scope of work changed as well. She had to work more overtime in order to provide him with the material to do his job. In her new position, she understood even more that her job was to make him look good. Marci knew she was in a supportive role. She was not to be the one in the spotlight, and she was thankful. But at times she had to deal with the feeling that her work was taken for granted. On her desk was a mini-plaque that reminded her of Jesus' words: "Blessed are the meek, for they will inherit the earth" (Matthew 5:5).

Your job may not be that of an assistant, but we're all called to assist. Not one of us is too great to help another. Having an attitude of humility will afford us a heart to serve and a desire to do all we can to meet the boss's needs. Doing our part to make him or her shine will eventually reflect positively on us.

Jesus described it as "Great Reversal: Many who are first will end up last, and the last first" (Mark 10:31, TM). You may need to give up something to make this happen, but God has promised that you'll be rewarded for it. In fact, you've been promised to inherit the earth. That's a pretty big payback!

Grace. . . Pray. . . Bless

Offer grace? I might if they will. Shawna remembers being raked over the coals for submitting a set of meeting minutes that her boss deemed substandard. There was also the time she was late for work because she had slept through her alarm. It seemed as if this boss held the opinion that mistakes equated incompetence. Slip-ups were not excused. Shawna struggled with the negative feedback and with trying to turn it around by offering grace in return. It was extremely difficult.

Pray? Can I pray that she gets hit by a bus? Okay—maybe that's a bit extreme. Christ tells us to pray for those who desire to do us harm. The heart of the issue is— will we pray that they succeed at work and that our hearts will be softened toward them? Those are tough words to pray, but if can pray for others, we'll be much less likely to slander or gossip about them.

Bless them? That's taking it too far. As we extend grace and pray that they receive God's love, we're praying a blessing over them. Throughout history, rulers, kings, and bosses have experienced God's favor because of the relationship their servant or employee had with the Almighty God (Genesis 30:27). Could this be why we're in this position? Does God desire to pour blessing through us into the lives and work of the boss?

If we believe this could be true, then we must make sure we're allowing God's blessing to flow through us. That's a pretty sobering thought. Maybe you *have* come to this position for such a time as this. Actually, God knew that you would be doing this job on this day and ordained that blessing would come to your boss through you. Speak the blessing from your heart, and then watch how God works in miraculous ways in the life of your boss, your workplace environment, and even your life.

Who's the Real Boss?

Who's the real boss anyway? No, it's not you. Our real boss is God. He's the one who gives us the strength to do our work and who orchestrates our lives. Nothing happens to us outside of God's knowledge or control. All our work is done for Him. When we find ourselves struggling in a work situation with a boss who makes life miserable, we must remember that God sees, cares, and is in control. His greater purpose may be to develop contentment in our hearts. Often the things that steal contentment can be a combination of things within our control. "Three of them are *lack of patience* (with God's timing), *lack of awareness* (of God's bigger picture), and *lack of skills* (to do the work that is required)."[2]

May we learn to trust God, that at exactly the right time He'll reward us for our service and bring down the proud. His timing is seldom the same as ours, but developing contentment in tough situations will develop the character we need not only to get through the situation but also to prepare us for the next. God's view of our circumstance is wider than we can comprehend, and He knows there's more at stake and more being worked out than we're aware of.

"Most people have trouble with about fifty percent of their bosses, so you have lots of company. Remember: you never stay with one boss that long; either he or she will move on, or you will. It may be best to try and wait it out; there will be reorganization shortly. Try to learn from the experience."[3]

If we're willing to be students—not only of our good relationships but of choosing to learn from the relationships that are tough and ragged—we'll come out stronger for having worked through our troubles. In the end, we'll be able to see the good that God brought about and resound with the psalmist, "Not to us, O LORD, not to us but to your name be the glory, because of your love and faithfulness" (Psalm 115:1).

Tenacity, patience, and contentment will build a relational bridge with even the toughest boss. We can choose to limp along with shoddy relational bridges, or we can do our best to create healthy connections with this person in authority over us. The choice is ours.

The Esther Connection

Esther had an attitude of submission and humility. Orphaned as a child, she went into her cousin Mordecai's home, where she was treated like his own daughter. As she was taken to the palace to enter the harem, she obeyed his instruction not to divulge her nationality. We're given no indication that she questioned Mordecai's directive, smugly thinking that it was ludicrous and unnecessary. Even after being made queen, she sought her older cousin's perspective and placed high value on his instruction.

Esther also displayed respect and honor to the king when she stated the protocol that must be followed—only summoned guests were allowed before the king. Even when she feared for her life, she remained respectful of the king's authority over her. I believe that it was Esther's humility and her respect for the man who was not only her husband but also the ultimate ruler God used to bring about the king's favor. In the end, blessing came to Esther and the kingdom, not so much because she was queen but because she was a woman who knew how to respond to the powers above her.

Verses to Study

Colossians 3:22-25

Romans 13:1-5
Ephesians 6:5-8
Philippians 2:3-8
Ecclesiastes 9:9-10
Matthew 7:12
Mark 10:31
Genesis 30:25-27
Psalm 115:1
Philippians 1:27-30

Questions for Reflection

1. In what ways has your heart been belligerent toward your boss that resulted in half-hearted work?

2. Think about the bosses you've had. What can you think of that you learned from these relationships? Ask God to use those experiences to make you more like Jesus.

3. Write a prayer of blessings for your boss. Continue to offer that to God; then watch for ways God blesses both the relationship and the work environment.

10 I Work with Him

Men and women are different. Well-known book titles give these differences an ethereal quality: *Men Are from Mars and Women Are from Venus* or *Women Are Spaghetti and Men Are Waffles.* From the sublime to the ridiculous, our differences are reinforced. All the hype about how different men are from women very often takes us down a path that describes not only our unique qualities but also quickly becomes a discussion about superiority.

Take for instance an online poll conducted by the British Broadcasting Corporation. It asked readers to post comments on the differences between men and women. The banter goes back and forth, but most telling is this comment by Paul from the UK: "Men enjoy publicizing their faults on BBC web sites; women enjoy publicizing men's faults on BBC web sites."[1] It seems we women can effortlessly take on the job of "official male-bashers." We'll attempt to buck that trend.

Workplace relationships with men are a reality. Rarely will one run across a female-only workplace environment. According to the United States Department of Labor, over forty-six percent of the workforce is women.[2] In Canada the ratio is over fifty percent.[3] In North America, statistics indicate that chances are about the same that we will work with a man as they are that we will work with a woman. A female nurse responded to my query for stories about working with men by stating that she had nothing to offer because she had never had a male coworker. She stopped herself when she realized that she worked alongside her husband on their family farm.

Whether it's a factor of nature or nurture, some women find it easier to be understood and more freeing to work alongside men. God has created each of us with a unique set of gifts. Letting go of stereotypes of men and women will enable us to celebrate our uniqueness; competition and fear will subside.

To make the most of these workplace relationships with men so that they neither hinder career advancement nor erode emotional and spiritual well-being, we should start by looking back.

History Influences the Future

A Chinese philosopher insisted on riding his mule backward so he would not be distracted by where he was going and could instead reflect on where he had been. The past for him was an important source of information, knowledge, and wisdom. Adlai Stevenson said, "You can chart your future more clearly and wisely when you know the path which led to the present."[4]

My training in counseling and my passion for spiritual formation have fueled my conviction that it's important to examine our past experiences. In my first book, *A Woman and Her Relationships,* I delved into Isaiah 51:1—"Listen to me, you who pursue righteousness and who seek the LORD: Look to the rock from which you were cut and to the quarry from which you were hewn." In order to have healthy workplace relationships with men, we must examine the roots of our attitudes.

The first thing an engineer must do when building a bridge is study the bedrock. By understanding the ground into which the foundation will be set, the civil engineer can create a bridge that takes into account both the strengths and inherent weakness of the quarry. In order to understand our responses to present circumstance and forge ahead into greater Christlikeness, we must examine our past experiences, then make the decision as to whether these experiences are treasure or trash. Without making this distinction, we'll perpetuate our past.

The next important step is to connect our past experiences to our present attitudes and behaviors. Often we project onto our present relationships our prejudices and hurts from the past. By rightfully identifying these, God can give us the strength to move beyond the stranglehold they have on us.

It's important to remember that history works the same way for the men with whom we work. We're the recipients of their learned responses to women. The women with whom they've worked over the years, their relationships with their mothers, and the health of their relationships with their wives or girlfriends will all impact their responses to you as a coworker.

Coming back to the bridge analogy, what happens upstream will guide the kind of bridge that is needed. For some men, their interaction with women—either in a familial or social setting—is strongly engrained, and they haven't been able to figure out how to treat a woman as a coworker. If your male coworker has a confrontational relationship with his wife in which yelling is fair play, he may be much more likely to bring that behavior into the workplace.

Relational protocol within the workplace means that men should not treat an older woman like a mother, a peer like a wife, or the new hire like a little sister.

Men will learn a lot about how to treat women as coworkers by what we teach them. Sheila was forging a new path in a leadership position as the first woman on an executive team. At her inaugural meeting her male boss asked if she would take notes. She realized that the men in the room were not accustomed to having a woman present at meetings unless she was a secretary. Sheila was going to have to retrain their thinking. Rather than getting disgruntled and snapping back, she simply stated, "I'll do it this time, but I expect that the responsibility will be shared with others at the next meeting or that a secretary will be brought in." She wasn't rude; she simply set out how she expected to be treated.

An additional factor that comes into play is that in most cases our male coworkers will have either a wife or girlfriend. Even though the relationship is professional and nothing remotely inappropriate has occurred, we may be seen as an "other woman" threat. The amount of time that a female coworker spends with her husband and the professional commonalities that are shared will play in to whether or not suspicion and contempt are directed our way. One wise woman said that when she gives as much attention as possible to the wife at company functions, it always comes back in a stronger and healthier relationship with her male coworker.

The degree to which we're aware of both our own heritage and that of our coworkers will position us to build bridges that will weather relational storms. Our pasts do not have to dictate our futures. We're all in a position to change our attitudes. There are many things we won't be able to change, but we do have a choice in the way we respond. The old adage that success is ten percent of what we were dished out in life and ninety percent what we do with it rings true in all relationships.

Diversity

As I polled women about what they liked about working with men, one of the most common responses was that working with men created an environment that was interesting and dynamic. Because men and women often approach situations from different vantage points, the opportunities to develop creative solutions are broadened. Dynamics become vibrant as diverse ideas are batted about.

Margaret was the only woman on a leadership team with five men. While it had taken her years to wade through her own sense of inferiority, her male counterparts' obvious acceptance of her equal voice at the table gave her the confidence to speak with the authority her expertise afforded. She had learned that it was her unique perspective that held greater sway than that of any one of the males in this environment. Often when the team found itself stalemated, it was her particular vantage point that offered the elusive solution.

Not only do coworkers or the team benefit from our female perspective, but there's also reciprocation for women who work alongside men. A well-known proverb says that "iron sharpens iron" (Isaiah 27:17). The potential exists for great personal growth to occur for women if they choose to learn from their male coworkers. This is where our hearts must be examined. Having a spirit of humility and openness to learning the way a man thinks and how he responds in situations will open a door to developing strengths that may otherwise remain untapped. It may be easier to work alongside a group of women who understand our unspoken sixth sense, but in so doing, the capacity for personal growth and unrealized potential may be thwarted. Working with men has the potential to make us better women if we seize the challenge.

Tell It Like It Is

I realize that I'm brushing up against dangerous territory when I make generalizations, because a man's personality will strongly dictate how he interacts with others. A choleric personality will tend to be strong and forceful. A sanguine will tend to be impulsive, saying what is on his mind and thinking later. A melancholy will generally put thought into the words he speaks and will proceed with precision. A man with a phlegmatic personality will often be calm and a peacemaker in his interactions.

Despite these differences, the responses I received from women in a wide variety of occupations reinforced the belief that women tend to see their male counterparts as being less calculating or manipulative than their female counterparts. As one woman put it, "Men can't be bothered to waste time on snits." To use another idiom, "What you see is what you get." Men tend to be seen as more straightforward and less likely to play emotional games or use double meanings in their speech. If men don't like something, they tell you. Men can have a rip-roaring argument, but as soon as they leave the boardroom, they're able to slap each other on the back, go out for lunch, and seemingly hold no grudges.

Women who are not intimidated by a man's directness have learned to stand their ground, go toe to toe, let go—or forgive and forget. Women who want to have strong working relationships with men must be able to learn from them by adopting a healthier way of dealing with disagreement or conflict that allows us not to take things personally and helps us stay more objective. Pride makes us resistant to learning from our male coworkers. Belligerence undermines the needed bridge for a healthy relationship.

Being aware of the positive results of working alongside men will affect your attitude. It's a relational trap to choose to see your male coworkers in a negative way. On the other hand, we can have a wonderfully positive attitude and still have to face the reality that there will be certain struggles because of the male-female disconnection. Let's take a look at some of these tough realities.

Harassment

I thought I might as well start with the worst-case scenario. There are men and women who can make the workplace unreasonably or illegally intolerable. They treat the workplace territorially and show disrespect for the rights of others. The label "workplace bully" is appropriate based on their behavior. Thankfully, most workplaces have come a long way in ensuring the physical *and* emotional well-being of all their employees, including zero tolerance for sexual, physical, and emotional harassment.

Denise, a young carpenter, spoke of an incident in which she had remained on a job site to finish a project after everyone else from her company had left. As she gathered her tools and prepared to leave, she noticed a group of painters were still on the job and that they were paying closer attention to her than to their painting. She felt panic rise within her as she realized that they stood between her and her truck. The volume of their cat calls was increasing. She quickly spied an escape route that would take her through a neighboring yard and around this group of jeering men. After that circumstance, she increased her vigilance to do all that she could to protect herself from such potentially dangerous workplace situations.

Another woman, Daphne, encountered harassment as the only woman on an otherwise all-male team of marketers in the grocery industry. To top it off, she was also the first woman of color to be in that position. The teasing and taunting that began on her first day on the job only intensified over time. One day while she was kneeling to set up a marketing display, a male coworker came and straddled his legs over her back. Acting out of a gut reaction, Daphne elbowed him in his groin (don't cheer too loudly!). As he buckled over, he spewed through clenched teeth, "I'm going to take you out." She was on her feet, ready to take on this bully who had harassed her one too many times. At that moment their supervisor stepped between them and said to her, "I'll never let a man touch a woman. I'll take care of this."

Harassment is never acceptable, nor is it ever the fault of the victim. Under no circumstance should inappropriate physical touch or sexual contact—or even the threat thereof—remain unreported. We must not allow harassment to continue unchecked. Our own safety and the safety of every other woman in that workplace are at stake. Let the harasser know that you want a specific behavior to stop. If you get no response, let your supervisor and human resources representative know about the situation.

Chauvinism

Chauvinism—the tendency for men to have a prejudiced belief that they're superior to women—can run very deep, particularly in certain occupations. Tracy, who worked in management for an oil and gas company, said that she felt that she has had to work much harder to have an equal voice with her male counterparts. She believe that she had to be stronger, smarter, and harder working than her male coworkers in order to prove herself to a predominantly male leadership. If this is the environment in which you work, what can be done?

First, accept the reality. If we simply remain disgruntled by the inequality, we end up putting our effort into bucking the trend rather than proving it wrong by being our best. The big egos around the table are much more fearful of being shown up by a woman than by their male peers. By letting them see our commitment to teamwork, we dispel their fear of competing with a woman. Having an open and collaborative approach will go much farther than being competitive.

Second, it's important for us to find our voices. The best definition I've found to describe this rather abstract concept comes from Nancy Beach's book *Gifted to Lead: The Art of Leading as a Woman in the Church.*[5] She quotes Jane Stephens, whose doctoral dissertation delved into the topic of the female voice. Here is Jane's description of finding one's voice:

> Voice goes two ways. It's about learning to get in touch, listen to and trust your own instincts; it's about threading instinct and experience into the fulcrum of sharp, clear expression. Born at the intersection of tenacity and certainty, it requires both vulnerability and presence. . . . Leaders need to find their own voices, their own best resources for being genuine in the midst of their organization, and they need to invite and to host the fullest presence of their colleagues. To have voice is to be fully present, to feel counted in, and counted on, to have something to say, and to be heard. The payoff for working in an organization in which everyone brings real voice to their work is a full measure of energy, balance, understanding and fun.[6]

Finding your voice does not mean getting louder, speaking with a deeper tone, or demanding your way. Those tactics will only reinforce a chauvinist's opinion. Rather, by embracing the way God created us with unique giftedness and competencies, we'll be able to speak with a clear and confident voice. If we feel the need to degrade men in order to elevate ourselves, we're guilty of reverse chauvinism. Take the higher road. Be confident in who you are in Christ, and allow that to flow into your relationships. Assurance will elicit respect, and that will combat chauvinism.

A third way to buck chauvinism is to be a woman of grace. Offering courtesy to someone who does not deserve it has the potential to disarm the natural sparring attitudes men espouse. Kindness, gentleness, goodness, self-control, and all the other fruit of the Spirit listed in Galatians 5:22-23 will disarm their preconceived opinions. Find ways to put men at ease. Step out of the combat zone. Be a leader of peace. Be a woman of grace.

The Fear of Being Too Feminine

Rachel had been in her new position only six weeks when she was confronted with a corporate issue that conflicted with her personal values. She knew her boss was a man of integrity, and she felt accepted by the otherwise all-male team; yet she dreaded having to approach them on this issue. She didn't fear their rebuttal. She didn't fear speaking her mind. What she feared was her inability to keep her emotions in check. As she went into the meeting, she vowed that she was not going to come across as the stereotypical hysterical, blubbering, emotional woman.

One of the challenges of working with men is that we may believe that we must leave our femininity at home. We take the stance that our femininity will be perceived disparagingly, or we berate ourselves that someone more competent would be able to keep their emotions in check. When emotion wells up around other women, we fear that they'll view us as being out of control, thus making us powerless against stronger, more conniving women. If we show emotion around men, we fear they'll see this as weakness, confirming that we're not able to run with the guys in a man's world. Therefore, we build a fortress around our emotions, not so much to keep others out but to keep our emotions under lock and key, fearing that if they escape, they have the power to undo the hard work of portraying ourselves as stalwart and competent.

Not only do we stuff our femininity, but we overcompensate by trying to be either asexual or masculine. One of Joy's hobbies was cooking. After a stressful day at work, she found it relaxing to come home and spend the evening baking. Her waistline had a hard time accommodating this hobby, so she decided to take her baking to the office. Joy found it discouraging when she brought these delicacies to be shared, and one of her female coworkers made the disparaging comment that she should get out of the kitchen, get a life, and stop being so domestic. On the other hand, a male colleague started calling her "Mom" despite the fact that he was older than Joy. Another male coworker made the derogatory comment that her baking confirmed that women were created to feed men. Eventually Joy stopped bringing these treats as it seemed that a number of her coworkers were unable to handle this aspect of who she was as a woman. She wondered what the comments would have been if one of the men in the office used his giftedness in cooking this way. She questioned that he would have suffered the same scorn.

When working with men, make sure you don't use emotion in such a way that it becomes a tool for manipulation. Crocodile tears are never appropriate, but allowing emotion to surface for those things that we strongly believe in does not make us a less valuable employee, a weaker boss, or an incompetent team player.

Wielding Feminine Power

Britney was only twelve years old when she discovered that her developing feminine body could be presented in such a way that it caught the attention of men. A life of promiscuity was not far off, and by the time Britney hit the floor as a well-endowed waitress, she reveled nightly in the power of her beauty.

We may smugly view ourselves as being a far cry from a cleavage-flaunting waitress, but we must drop any sense of self-righteousness. The clothes we choose to wear or our flirtatious attitudes and actions can be a subconscious wielding of sexual power. As one woman aptly declared, "It must be hard to work with a woman professionally when her cleavage is staring at you!" May we have the humility to ask God how we're guilty of using our sexuality to wield power over men in the workplace.

Sexual and Emotional Integrity

The topic of sexual integrity within the workplace is seldom talked about. Even within our churches it's often minimized or sidelined as something that really isn't a problem.

The reality is, though, that there *is* a problem. Even if we're good church ladies, not one of us is immune. Scripture says, "You're not exempt. You could fall flat on your face as easily as anyone else" (1 Corinthians 10:12, TM).

The workplace has become the number-one place where married people meet someone with whom they engage in infidelity. The old stereotype about the boss and the young secretary carrying on an affair has been overshadowed by an increasing number of peers who become romantically involved. Extramarital or premarital infidelity with a coworker is not uncommon; it happens frequently. Seldom does a woman get up in the morning with the intent to engage in sexual flirtation or sexual activity with a coworker that day, but it transpires insidiously at an alarming rate. So what must we do to keep ourselves pure?

The answer starts a long way from the bedroom. Sexual purity in the workplace begins when we make small compromises that on their own seem insignificant but when brought together take us to a place that's very different from sexual integrity. We may resist having an actual affair with a coworker, but we'll still have crossed the line into infidelity when we allow our emotions and thoughts to propel us to think about him in a way that should be reserved only for our husband. Jesus spoke directly to this when he said, "You have heard that it was said, 'Do not commit adultery.' But I tell you that anyone who looks at a woman lustfully has already committed adultery with her in his heart" (Matthew 5:27-28). That principle holds true for women looking lustfully at men as well.

Shannon Ethridge has written a helpful book on this topic titled *Every Woman's Battle*, which explores the pursuit of sexual and emotional integrity. I want to share one section from her book that will hopefully whet your appetite to read more. More important, may it convict your heart that this is a personal concern that deeply affects our workplace relationships.

You are getting into a four-door car by yourself. It's late at night and you are in a rough neighborhood. In order to feel safe, what is the first thing you are going to do when you get in the car? Right. Lock the doors.

How many doors will you lock? You may think this is a silly question, but think about it. If you only locked one or two or even three of the doors, would you be safe? Of course not. All four doors must be locked to keep out an unwelcome intruder.

The same is true with keeping out unwelcome sexual temptation. These temptations can invade our lives and eventually give birth to sin in four ways. The thoughts we choose to entertain in our minds can influence us. The words we speak or the conversations we engage in can lure us down unrighteous, dangerous paths. So can the failure to guard our hearts from getting involved in unhealthy relationships. And when we allow our bodies to be in the wrong place at the wrong time with the wrong person, we can be led toward sexual compromise.[7]

We must guard our hearts and minds around emotional integrity in order to have sexual integrity. By ensuring that all four doors are locked—our thoughts, the words we speak, guarding against unhealthy relationship, and keeping our bodies out of places they shouldn't be—we can win this battle.

It's important to consider what leads us into this danger zone. Why do we choose not to lock all the doors? Seeking attention and approval feeds our self-esteem. Often if approval is lacking, we attempt to substitute illicit attention to soothe a very real need. If we did not receive the love and attention we desired from our fathers, we may feel a deep need to somehow receive that attention from other sources.

Darlene remembers when she was a little girl working many hours on a science project that earned her the best mark in her class. When she raced home to show her professor father the well-deserved accolades, his response was cool, simply pointing out where she could have been more current in the statistics she had used. She recalls leaving his office with a sense of despondency that she would never be good enough.

Darlene has come to realize that this unmet need for her father's approval causes her to sidle up to her male coworkers. Their praise and attention to her competency have caused her to give herself emotionally to these men. She realizes how she melts like butter in response to her smooth-talking and complimentary male colleagues.

Annette realizes that she's in the danger zone when a male co-worker comments on how nicely she's dressed. It doesn't take too many comments from this particular man in her department about how particularly beautiful she looks that day or that she seems to have a certain glow about her before she starts to choose her outfits based on her desire to elicit compliments from him. The slippery slope is greased by her husband's lack of appreciation of these same outfits. These women may not have been able to get their emotional needs met by father or husband, but they're both in a position to stop their inappropriate and incessant search for affirmation from male coworkers.

From my study of the personalities and their effect on marriages, I've observed a trend. The danger to our marriages is seldom a man who has a personality similar to our husband. I am a *sanguine,* and my husband is a *melancholy,* and I really have no desire to have another man in my life who's so different from me. I know that my guard has to be that much more secure when I'm around men who are different from my husband and more like me. I'm at greatest risk with a guy who is a sanguine, because he's fun-loving, outgoing, and naturally speaks my emotional language. The risks to our marriages are not contained to just similar personalities; appropriate boundaries must be maintained at all times with all men, despite their personalities. Our natural bent screams to the contrary, but if we're to follow God's ways, we must guard our hearts and minds to guard our marriages.

Our God-given sexuality has an amazing purpose that's good and satisfying within the proper bounds of marriage. Outside of marriage, it's destructive. Don't play with fire. You may get away with it a few times, but destruction will come. I've never met a godly woman who has come to the end of her career and has said, "If only I had had that affair! Life really would have worked out better."

No. The opposite roars from the voice of the experienced. Protect yourself. Save your career. Honor the temple of God, which is your body. Keep in check the passions that surge through your body. The workplace is no place for affairs—either sexual or emotional.

So how do we do this? We must allow God to search our hearts. King David knew all too well the outcome of wrong thoughts. His lack of emotional integrity led to the sinful action in his affair with Bathsheba. Confessing his sin, he wrote, "Search me, O God, and know my heart; test me and know my anxious thoughts. See if there is any offensive way in me" (Psalm 139:23). Our attempt to hide our thoughts and motives from God is pointless; He already knows them, and He loves us and wants better for us. Opening up to God and allowing Him to infuse you with His love will give you the strength to turn off this path of sin.

A next step should be to confess our struggle to our husband. This can be incredibly difficult. We may fear his response, or we may desire to shelter him from hurt. These can be valid concerns. But ultimately, if we're going to have marriages that are healthy, we're going to need the accountability that comes with being honest. Unfortunately, many women do not have the level of trust or openness in their marriages that would allow them to feel safe to share the struggle. At the very least, we must have someone we trust in whom we can confide. We need to be able to tell someone who will hold us accountable to a higher standard rather than someone who would sympathize to the point of approving of our actions.

Last, we must set boundaries and practice. Know what our limits are, and don't budge on them. Elaine was attracted to a coworker and enjoyed his reciprocating friendship. As their friendship deepened, she became increasingly aware of what happened in her heart during their lunches together. She knew she was treading on dangerous ground and set about to tighten the boundaries that would preserve emotional integrity. She thought through how she was going to respond the next time they got together for lunch. When they met at the restaurant—which she later realized was part of the problem, as it felt like a date and they were both married—she would extend her hand to give a hearty shake and use her left hand to squeeze his shoulder before he could embrace her. She was also prepared to make an off-the-cuff comment that she had decided to save all her hugs for her husband. The first time was a bit awkward, but they laughed it off. Simply by mentioning her husband, she showed she wanted to esteem her husband's place in her life and set new stricter boundaries. The discomfort Elaine felt that day was much easier than what could have developed if she had allowed her feelings to go unchecked.

You might think this was a rather extreme example, but another woman, a top executive at a multinational firm—and the only woman at this executive level—had to put safeguards in place when she went on business trips. It was her practice to join the "guys" when they went out for dinner, but she made the choice early in her career to avoid becoming involved in the revelry that characterized the after-dinner gatherings. Yes, she was going back to an empty hotel room, and, yes, she would rather have stayed and enjoyed the fun, but she knew she might be compromised if she stayed.

Whether we need to set tighter boundaries on our thoughts and emotions or we need to change our interactions with our male co-workers, our relationships will be healthier as a result. Scripture exhorts us not even to have a hint of sexual immorality. "Don't allow love to turn into lust, setting off a downhill slide into sexual promiscuity, filthy practices, or bullying greed" (Ephesians 5:3, TM). Let's not stoop to the standards around us that would have us opening the door to relationships that are not pure in action or thought. We need to hold ourselves to a very high standard. Anything less is unbefitting of a beautiful woman created in the image of God and loved passionately by Him.

The Esther Connection

Esther was part of a male-dominated society in which the power of the Persian Empire lay in the hands of the king, his male advisors, and his right-hand man, Haman. When Vashti, Esther's predecessor, refused to display her womanly beauty to King Xerxes and his guests, she was banished as queen. And yet it was Esther's femininity that God used to place her in the role where He wanted her to be "for such a time as this." Esther's feminine charms and beauty caused her to find favor with the king.

I find it interesting that Esther utilized the realm of her womanhood to invite Xerxes and Haman to a banquet she had prepared where she would reveal the destitution of the Jewish people and her Jewish heritage. She could have spoken her mind in the royal court, or she could have waited to meet the king in the royal bedroom, but instead, she unashamedly operated out of her femaleness.

Ladies, let's not dismiss or decrease the fact that God has brought each of us to be women in our place of work. If He wanted a man, he would have chosen someone else. Being afraid to be all that God created us to be, feeling that we must be either less than or different than our true selves in order to work alongside men, diminishes the impact we could have. Let's be an Esther, who, even though she was surrounded by powerful men, was fully a woman and fully used by God.

The Last Word

A whole book could have been written about the topic of working with men, but I've tried to condense it into one chapter. As I researched, listened to women's stories, and pondered this topic, I realized afresh that although working with men may have its unique challenges, it really comes back to this: if we're going to have healthy workplace relationships, we have to learn to build the appropriate bridges to these men. And how do we do that? Be a leader at your workplace by treating the men around you with respect and grace, even if they don't deserve it. We have the opportunity to be a conduit of God's grace and love in our workplace, or we can choose to set aside these gifts from God and become unfeminine, conniving, or an irritant. Be a woman of integrity in every relationship, and in doing so you'll teach the men you work with how you want to be treated.

Verses for Study

Isaiah 51:1
Proverbs 27:17
Galatians 5:22-23
2 Samuel 11
1 Corinthians 10:12-13
Matthew 5:27-30
Psalm 139:23-24
Ephesians 5:3-7

Questions for Reflection

1. What experiences have you had working alongside men? What positive impressions of working with men did you accumulate? What happened during these experiences that has tainted your viewpoint of working with men?

2. Do the clothes you wear to work accentuate your sexuality? Do you watch to see if your femininity is a draw to the men with whom you work? How do you respond to flirting?

3. Are there changes in your attitude and actions that should be made so that you can be a woman of integrity in your relationship with your male coworkers? What are those changes?

11 I Work with Her

"**I**'d rather work with ten men than with one woman."

These words unfortunately reflect a sentiment commonly shared by women. It makes me wonder what's happening within the hearts of women that makes us so hard to work with. Why do we find it difficult to build healthy workplace relationships with other women?

Before we delve into the challenges of working alongside women, it's important to note that female coworkers are not always our foes. Sometimes they can become our best friends. Many women I interviewed talked about colleagues who were supportive and encouraging and who made their workplace a truly pleasurable experience. Building healthy relationships with the women we work with can become one of the greatest joys associated with our jobs. Even if deep and lasting friendships are not the outcome, our goal should be to have relationships that are God-pleasing and healthy.

The emphasis of this chapter is to look at building healthy relationships with other women even if the connection is less than ideal. Experience whispers to our subconscious that other women may not be trustworthy, that they're our rivals, so we either protect or promote ourselves. Women use many tactics to protect themselves emotionally from perceived rivals in the workplace.

Quarantine the Nemesis

When a hospital patient is discovered with strong bacteria, the carrier is quarantined to isolate and eradicate the problem. We women do this with each other. If a female coworker is seen as a threat, one of the most effective ways to diminish her impact is to isolate her. We may be powerless to curtail her movement in and out of our workplace, but we're certainly capable of creating emotional barriers by keeping her out of conversations, e-mail threads, or even group events. Then we feign ignorance to falsify our innocence.

We make an assessment that a colleague has infiltrated the inner circle to benefit her own position. When she enters the staff room, we simply ignore her by turning toward each other, lowering our voices, and avoiding eye contact. She quickly catches on that she's not welcome in our lunchroom chatter. We may even build walls between ourselves and those we've come to believe are somehow different from us. However, they may be much like us and exhibit qualities we wish we had. We either don't like them, or we see them as a threat, so we quarantine them from our lives and hearts.

Barbara had received a long-sought-for promotion, but it came at the cost of relationships. For a number of years she had worked long hours beside two other female engineers in her department. Barbara would have described their relationship as a semblance of sisterhood. But when it was announced that she had received this promotion and was to become the new team lead, walls went up between her and the "sisters." She would see the other two going out for lunch, realizing she had not been invited. A coolness developed between them and her. Jealousy fed the notion that she was now on the other side and had become an adversary instead of a friend.

Predator on the Loose

When you see the word *predator,* you probably think of a carnivorous animal out to devour its prey. Or maybe you have images of a male stalker, crouching in the bushes, waiting to pounce on an innocent passerby. Expand that definition to include women who use their words to kill the reputation of a coworker. This was one of the most frequent and emphatic reasons that women gave for not wanting to work with other women. Slander, backstabbing, and gossip run rampant in the workplace, and women appear to be the chief perpetrators.

Slander occurs when one makes a false and defamatory statement about another. It's one of the offenses we're to avoid in the Ten Commandments (Exodus 20:16). Christ called it murder: "You're familiar with the command to the ancients, 'Do not murder.' I'm telling you that anyone who is so much as angry with a brother or sister is guilty of murder. Carelessly call a brother 'idiot!' and you just might find yourself hauled into court. Thoughtlessly yell 'stupid!' at a sister and you are on the brink of hellfire. The simple moral fact is that words kill" (Matthew 5:21-22, TM).

Sylvia knew it was wrong to make such a malicious inference about the receptionist, but she justified it by rationalizing that she had just hinted at this woman's impropriety. Unfortunately, once the words left her mouth, she saw that they were picking up speed, and before long there was a whole wave of backlash against this innocent woman. Full of regret, Sylvia would have loved to take back those words that had been spoken out of anger and envy, but once they had left her mouth, she could never undo the murderous effect on her coworker's character that had been caused by her slander.

Backstabbing occurs when we attack someone unfairly, especially in an underhanded or deceitful manner. Rhonda had left her profession as a confident emergency room nurse but reentered, after nine years at home with her young children, as a refresher student on a medical unit. She felt overwhelmed by the learning curve; even worse was the demeaning and unsupportive environment created by the much-younger "senior" staff. Fear of inadequacy engulfed Rhonda as she observed the mocking and eye-rolling and heard the derogatory remarks that cut like knives. She wondered what they said about her when she wasn't around.

Gossip, which is talking about or rumoring about the private or personal affairs of others, may seem like a tame cousin compared to these other two forms of malicious talk, but its insidious nature and prevalence in the workplace makes it just as dangerous. Gossip has become an accepted means of bonding between women.

In her book *Mean Girls All Grown Up,* Hayley DiMarco has this to say about gossip:

> For women, gossip is the currency that buys us a place in another woman's heart. It's bonding. You know the feeling. When you tell a friend something you heard or saw and you know you shouldn't be repeating it, you feel the endorphins running though your blood, almost giving you a little buzz. It's a great feeling, and the two of you become soul sisters.[1]

DiMarco goes on to say that gossip has become the preferred weapon of choice in defamation against others.

> Gossip makes them feel good and others feel bad; it's a perfect weapon containing both pleasure and pain. Its destructive powers are stronger than its pleasure could ever be.[2]

Scripture says this about gossip: "What dainty morsels rumors are—but they sink deep into one's heart" (Proverbs 18:8, NLT). "Gossip separates close friends" (Proverbs 16:28).

Self-Promotion

When we feel threatened, one of the tactics we try is to pull ourselves up to a higher position. Ego, coming from that inner drive to be recognized and satisfied, is one of the strongest forces in life. In attempts to build up our position, we clamor to rise above our coworkers, but in so doing we often knock down someone else. Our goal is seldom to level the playing field. Rather, the goal becomes to get the other person off the field. Self-promotion becomes the means by which we do this.

Scripture describes it as "pushing your way to the front or sweet-talking your way to the top" (Philippians 2:3, TM). More traditional versions use the terminology "selfish ambition or vain conceit" (Philippians 2:3).

Joseph M. Stowell offers this explanation of *vain conceit*: "The words for *vain conceit* come from two Greek words meaning 'empty and glory.' Vain conceit is the glorification of emptiness—the promotion of our 'zeroness.'"[3]

Exalting ourselves expands as we experience the exhilaration of feeling better or more highly esteemed than we truly are. Pride is a master with a voracious appetite, always wanting to be one notch higher. We don't like to use this word to describe ourselves, but many of us are guilty of being a braggart, boasting about things we did not honestly impact or making promises we cannot deliver. Similarly, when we flatter, we often do so to elicit reciprocal positive comments. Flattery "puts others in debt to our positive comments about them."[3] Exaggeration stretches the truth. For fisherman or boardroom executives, making things even slightly better than reality gives us an upper hand against the competition.

These scenarios—self-protection, isolation, malicious words, and self-promotion—are all potent destroyers of relationships. In effect, if you want to blow up your workplace relationships, particularly with women, you now have a bomb-building kit. However, I feel confident that you did not pick up this book to learn how to destroy relationships. In reality, we don't need to read books to learn how to destroy relationships; we seem rather adept at that simply because of our sin nature that reeks havoc on the way we connect with others. So now that we know what we don't want to do, let's look at the heart issues that will set us on the course of building healthy relationships.

We Are the Perpetrators

Before we get too self-righteous and start to identify all the women around us who are "mean girls,"[5] let's be honest with ourselves. There are times when we're the perpetrators of self-protection, isolation, malicious words, and self-promotion.

I could make a blanket statement that it's a heart issue, but without further examination, that seems like a shallow explanation. If we receive a diagnosis from our physician that we have coronary heart disease, we must take a look at the patterns of eating and exercise that have led to this heart problem. That's what we need to do in regard to our relationships, by looking at what we're doing to contribute to the heart issues that cause relational breakdown. This must happen before we can administer the corrective measure.

Identifying the experiences throughout life that shape our thinking and thus influence our behavior is not just good psychology—it's considering the quarry from which you've been cut (Isaiah 51:1-2). Looking at our pasts, identifying the patterns of relating that we perpetuate, and discerning which ones are leading to destruction of relationships rather than building healthy connections is essential when it comes to our relationships with other women in the workplace. We need to ask God to show us why we're aggressive toward certain women, why we feel they're a threat. Each one of us must pray, "Investigate my life, O God, find out everything about me; Cross-examine and test me, get a clear picture of what I'm about" (Psalm 139:23, TM). We must be able to identify our behaviors that contribute to the breakdown in relationships.

Being on the Receiving End

Every day Jenny shows up at her teaching job knowing that she could be on the receiving end of what she calls a "Betty blast." Betty has a reputation of being a spiteful, mean woman who displays bipolar behavior. One minute she can be pleasant and giving you a hug—the next you're met with an icy verbal blast. One morning Jenny arrived in their shared classroom to find two posters torn off the wall and strewn across Jenny's desk. When Jenny asked if the posters had bothered her, Betty's icy response was "Yes," with no further explanation. Jenny took all the proactive steps of asking Betty what she was doing that was causing her such discontent and if there were any changes that could be made that would make Betty's life easier. Betty didn't offer an explanation but simply walked away from the conversation.

As time went on, Jenny realized the problem was not hers. Betty was bent on interacting in anger and selfishness. Jenny had confronted the problem and then had to make the decision to let go of her attempts to change Betty. She was following the biblical principle of "If it is possible, as far as it depends on you, live at peace with everyone" (Romans 12:18). Jenny could not control Betty, but she could control her own response.

When *She* Is an Enemy

An enemy is an opponent whose hostility poses a threat. During His time on earth, Jesus was surrounded by enemies, including Satan, the ultimate enemy. So what does Scripture tell us to do with our enemies? What can we bring into our relationship with an enemy so that the erosive nature of his or her actions does not destroy us and can instead be reversed to build a relational bridge? Our solution has four parts, which are summed up in Luke 6:27-28: "Love your enemies, do good to those who hate you, bless those who curse you, pray for those who mistreat you."

Love your enemies.

Even though Christ had many people hating Him, not the least of whom were the religious leaders who should have supported Him but instead pushed public opinion to have Him killed, Christ showed nothing to them but love. At times He got angry as He spoke truth, but He always did so in love. The ultimate evidence of His love was His willingness to die on the Cross so that the very people who sent Him there could be reconciled to the Father. Is there any greater evidence of love than to lay down your life for someone? Can we love our enemies like that? Not on our own.

Love and hate are antitheses; but isn't that typical of God's kingdom? Where human nature would turn away from enemies, God's nature is to move into that hatred and diffuse it with love. Love is the overarching approach we are called to use with our enemies. The next three parts of this antidote give instruction as to *how* we can show love.

Do good to those who hate you.

"If your enemy is hungry, feed him; if he is thirsty give him something to drink" (Romans 12:20). Kindness disarms hostility. Jesus' words to His followers were to "Live generously and graciously towards others" (Matthew 5:48, TM). The parable of the Good Samaritan illustrated the true meaning of kindness (Luke 10:25-37). Living a life that's generous toward others will bring kindness and benevolence into the workplace.

Bless those who curse you.

When we bless someone, we're asking God to make good things happen to and for them. Our human condition would tell us to repay evil with evil, but Christ's way is to repay curses with blessings. When given a chance to say something unkind about someone, especially someone we know has been spreading slander about us, we can choose to find something good to say about him or her, or we follow our mother's adage "If you can't say something nice about a person, don't say anything at all."

Pray for those who mistreat you.

Jesus was breathing His last on the Cross, but His words gave evidence to His teachings. "Father, forgive them, for they know not what they are doing" (Luke 23:34). Stephen, while being stoned for his passion for Jesus, spoke these words as the rocks flew at him: "Lord, do not hold this sin against them" (Acts 7:59). Coming before God in prayer allows Him the opportunity to transplant our bruised egos with a heart focused on Him. Praying also then turns our focus to God rather than the mistreatment we've received at the hands or words of others. True heart change will occur when we can start praying.

Quite the Outcome

Teresa could tell from her first day in the department that this work environment was going to be a challenge. The supervisor was a lifetime employee who had worked his way up the ranks and paid little attention to what was actually happening on the front end. In his mind, if his twenty female employees showed up to work and got the shipments sent on time, he didn't care what office politics developed. As long as he didn't have to put up with whining women in his office, how they interacted was not his problem.

Teresa was shown around the maze of cubicles by a friendly young woman who seemed to know everything about everyone. As they moved past each person's workspace, tidbits of information were shared. Some were useful suggestions on how to get along with that person; others were clearly juicy morsels of gossip. When they walked past the corner desk, her guide whispered in a hushed tone, "This is Carol's desk. Watch your step. Don't ever cross her. Even though she's at the same level as you and me, everyone, including her, knows that she's the real boss. I've found it best to just keep my distance."

As Teresa pondered this warning, she realized the fear and anxiety welling up within her. *Will I be able to keep my distance from Carol? Will I be able to stay in her good graces? Simply by being the new kid on the block, am I already at a disadvantage, pegged for attacks by her?* There were so many unknown scenarios stirring up fear.

The one thing that Teresa did know was that she was going to need God's help in ways she had never experienced before. Somewhat resigned, yet refusing to let hope dwindle, Teresa went about setting up her desk. Next to her telephone she set out the picture frame with her kids' photo and the caption "With God all things are possible." She smiled as she reflected on the miraculous adoption of her two children that had proven this to be true.

Later that afternoon as Teresa was working on her first assignment, a quiet but intense voice spoke over her shoulder. "So you're the newbie. You've probably already had the official tour, but let me give you an inside tip. Do your own work, don't come looking for favors, mind your own business, and don't bother trying to be our friend. Oh, and one last piece of advice: don't shove your God stuff down our throats." As quickly as she had appeared, she was gone.

Teresa sat, shaken and stunned by what had just transpired. Carol's last statement was the most unnerving. How had she known that she was a Christian? She felt around her neck and realized she was wearing her customary cross necklace, but then her eyes fell to the photo frame, and she felt like weeping. Had this been enough to set off such a strong response from the office bully? Teresa wiped a tear from the corner of her eye.

That night, as was her habit, Teresa reflected on her day and asked God to show her where her words, actions, and attitudes had pleased Him and where He had been grieved. Immediately Carol came to mind. The Holy Spirit impressed upon Teresa's heart that the fear she was experiencing was a natural response to the unknown events of a known adversary and that He was calling her to live a life that would overcome this fear. As she recalled a verse, "Perfect love drives out fear" (1 John 4:18), Teresa prayed that God would show her ways and give her opportunities to show love to all her coworkers, but especially to Carol.

As the weeks turned into months, Teresa was the brunt of many unfair practices and insinuations. She was accused of being a "dogooder" who was too soft on clients. Although her work had been declared exemplary when reviewed by the supervisor, it was ridiculed and revamped when it passed through her colleagues, causing her extra work. Teresa had initially tried to show interest in people by asking questions and celebrating who they were and how well they did their jobs, but she always seemed to be rebuffed. Everything within her wanted to stay at her desk and eat lunch alone, but she felt God's gentle nudge to go to the lunchroom. If she was excluded from the conversation, it meant she had more time to pray for the women around her.

If Teresa had been trying to pass on kindness and blessing to her coworkers of her own volition, it would have dwindled that first week. As she prayed for strength and love, she started noticing some changes in her "enemies." At first it seemed that the taunting, ridicule, and antagonism increased, but Teresa was determined that she had been placed at this job "for such a time as this." She was not going to get caught up in their snare of negativity, nor was she going to let them ruin her job.

A few women who were also sidelined by Carol and her cronies started turning to Teresa for encouragement. Initially they tried to engage Teresa in hazing directed toward Carol, but Teresa would not participate. Instead, she found positive things to say about Carol's quality of work and her punctuality. When someone made note that she had "inadvertently" been left off the lunch sign-up sheet, Teresa brushed it off and gave her "enemies" the benefit of the doubt. She was determined to go to work each day and interact with her coworkers in a way that was pleasing to Jesus. On her way to work she prayed that she would be able to be the same type of coworker that Jesus would be if He were a woman in that office.

One side benefit that Teresa experienced was a promise made by Jesus in Matthew 5:45. As He was telling His disciples to love their enemies, He slipped in this statement: "Let them bring out the best in you, not the worst" (TM). Teresa could attest to this. Despite the toxic environment of her office, she had peace and joy. There were days when she dreaded facing the relational trials, but she also realized the growth in her own life. Her trust and dependence on God had never been this strong. She was excelling in her job responsibilities, and her interest and care for her coworkers was exhilarating rather than draining. She had taken on her enemy, not in an aggressive attempt to annihilate her but rather through winning the war with love.

One event in Carol's life changed the trajectory of this office and the people who worked there. When her daughter was in a serious car accident, Carol ended up missing three weeks of work. Teresa saw this as part of an answer to her prayer. No, she hadn't been praying that Carol would be hit by a bus, but she had been praying that something significant would happen so that Carol could truly experience God's love. So Teresa set about flooding Carol's life with kindness, blessing, and love.

Teresa was the first to go to some of her coworkers, particularly those who had suffered under the brunt of Carol's meanness, and suggest that they pick up Carol's workload during this time. Several of the women were dumbfounded that it would be Teresa, the lowest of rank in Carol's eyes, who would initiate this kindness.

When it was discovered that Carol was spending day and night at the hospital and that her two younger children were struggling to keep things going at home, Teresa organized meals to be brought to their home.

When Carol finally arrived back at work and the information leaked out that the medical bills had exceeded their insurance, Teresa saw this as one more opportunity to bless her coworker and sent around an envelope for people's contributions to help alleviate this financial burden.

Carol had been back to work for a while, but she looked bedraggled. One morning as Teresa was praying for Carol, a thought came of a new way to bless her. She went and bought a gift certificate to a spa and slipped it in Carol's coat pocket with a typed note so her handwriting couldn't be identified: "You've had such a hard two months. Enjoy your massage."

After lunch, the familiar quiet and intense voice spoke over Teresa's shoulder. "Why did you do it? Why have you been so nice to me when I've been so mean to you?"

Teresa took a second to shoot a prayer heavenward asking for direction, and as she swirled her chair around, she caught a glimpse of her photo frame—"With God all things are possible."

"From my first day here, I've known you didn't like me. I didn't know why, and actually it doesn't really matter. I know that there's a reason I'm in this job, and it has to do with more than just doing the work. I'm here to show love and kindness to those around me. I won't deny that there have been times when you've made it difficult to come to work, but I've kept coming and kept praying for you and for each of the women in this department. When your daughter was in the accident, I saw it as an opportunity to pass on kindness to you in your time of need. No agenda, just love."

Teresa could see the glistening in Carol's eyes that belayed her tough exterior. From pursed but quivering lips, Carol said a simple "Thank you," and then she left. There was no fanfare, no hugs, and no statements that Teresa's love had changed her life. Just a simple thanks, yet Teresa knew that Carol had been changed. God's love had gotten into her heart, and she would never be the same.

From that day forward, even though Carol's crusty exterior was still intact, her heart was different. The slander lessened, the cruel insinuations ceased, and she seemed to be more subdued. When Teresa left that job two years later, not much had changed outwardly. Carol had always kept Teresa at bay; they had never had a heart-to-heart conversation, but Teresa left knowing that her presence had impacted that office and the hearts of her female coworkers in a very significant way. The only tool that effectively builds relationships with difficult people is God's love. "These three remain: faith, hope and love. But the greatest of these is love" (1 Corinthians 13:13).

The Esther Connection

Only two references to Esther's relationships with other women are made in Scripture. The first occurs when she's initially brought to the palace and put under the care of Hegai, the eunuch who was in charge of the harem. We're told that Esther pleased Hegai and won his favor. He assigned her seven maids selected from the king's palace and moved her and her maids into the best place in the harem (Esther 2:9).

From this part of the narrative we know that Esther was likely surrounded by women. She had other women with whom she was competing to gain the attention of the king, and she also had women who were at her beck and call to provide for her needs, making her the best she could be.

Imagine if we were in that scenario. It represents a recipe for backbiting, slander, envy, and all malicious talk. Although we're given no glimpse into how these female relationships evolved, the second reference to Esther's relationship with women points to the fact that she had risen above this female tendency.

After Mordecai convinced Esther that she must go to the king in hopes of saving the Jewish race, she tells Mordecai to gather the Jews of Susa together and to spend the next three days fasting and praying. She ends her response to Mordecai by assuring him that she and her maids would fast as well (Esther 4:16).

Even if your coworkers don't have the same beliefs as you, have you built relationships with them that would allow you to be real with them? I believe that's the example Esther gives us. In her time of greatest need, she's able to go to her maidens and ask that they join her in preparation to go before the king. It took courage, but it also took many months of building trust so that when her need was great, the relational bridges were in place.

Verses for Study

Matthew 5:21-22
Proverbs 18:8-9
Romans 12:18-21
Luke 10:25-37
Matthew 5:43-48
Luke 6:27-28
1 Samuel 1:1-19
1 John 4:16-18
Matthew 25:34-46
1 Corinthians 13:13

Questions for Reflection

1. Did you have a sister with whom you were compared and always found wanting? Did your mother make you feel that you never lived up to her expectations?

2. What friendships do you have in which much of the talk is about outward appearances and comparisons?

3. In your relationships with female coworkers, what heart changes must you make so that you can love them, do good to them, and bless them?

12 Sharing Your Faith

Let's pretend that you've been given a new assignment. You'll be packing up your office, home, and relationships and moving to Timbuktu. No, this is not just a legendary place in the middle of nowhere. It's an actual city in Mali, West Africa. You've been assigned to live among the Tuaregs, a nomadic desert tribe, best known for headdress and camel herds. You'll be setting up a business in the neighborhood, employing local workers, eating at the local restaurants, and joining the Timbuktu Chamber of Commerce. Your mission is to learn as much as you can about the Tuareg culture so that you can effectively love the people. You're not there to try to get them to change—you're simply called to love. Will you take up the challenge?

Some may be intrigued by both the challenge and adventure of this opportunity, but it's unlikely that I'll get many takers for this isolated assignment in Africa. How often have you heard someone express the fear that if he or she gives God control of his or her life, He might send him or her to be a missionary in Africa? Thoughts of leaving behind hot running water and flush toilets can be as big a stumbling block as having to say good-bye to aging parents at the airport.

What if I told you that your assignment is not to go to Africa but that you're simply being asked to stay at your present workplace? You're to interact with the people in the cubicles around you or with those who work beside you on the assembly line. Your assignment includes making sure that you spend time with your coworkers over lunch, showing them genuine interest and compassion. Every chance you get, you're to show your coworkers that you care about them and what's happening in their lives. You're not demanding them to change either their values or their lifestyles; you're simply to show heartfelt care and authentic love to those with whom you work. Is that a challenge you'll take?

Not one of us would diminish the importance of moving to Africa to love the Tuaregs, but how many of us would see the value of living out our faith by loving our coworkers? All of us who have put our faith in Jesus Christ have calls upon our lives to pass on to others the love that He has so freely given us. When love is hoarded, it becomes pungent. If passed on, it becomes a beautiful aroma.

The first amendment of the United States Constitution decrees that church and state be separated. This has made its way into the workplace to such a degree that many of us feel we must check our faith at the door. Being a Christian may not be politically correct; talking about our faith may even be taboo. But sharing our faith may spell career suicide. So how can we maintain the expectations of the workplace while living out Christ's mandate to be witnesses not only to the ends of the earth but also to our "Jerusalem" workplace? (Acts 1:8).

I believe the responsibility to share our faith is a privilege that's earned through authenticity and love. None do more harm to the cause of Christianity than the Bible thumpers, pious Christians, and hellfire-and-brimstone preachers using the workplace as a platform to preach rather than a place to sincerely love. A damning God portrayed through a pharisaical attitude only deepens resistance. God's love woos and breaks down walls.

This Is Not a Project

It's imperative that we not view our unbelieving coworkers as "projects." Many of us have been taught that we have to go get people saved. This conjures up the image of pulling a straggly mule to a watering hole while muttering "Come on, you stubborn animal. You need this water."

Probably all of us have experienced being pushed to do something by someone with a less-than-loving motive. And it's a common reaction to resist as soon as we're feeling forced to do something. If a salesman tries to draw us in by saying, "Have I got a deal for you!" we immediately become skeptical. That's how it is when our coworkers feel that Christianity is being forced down their throats.

We must check our hearts and examine our motives. Are we simply trying to score a conversion, or is our desire to love our colleagues?

Maybe you're bristling at that because you decidedly do not love your coworkers. You may not even like them. In the first chapter I interchanged the word *love* with *care* and developed the idea that as God's love pours into you it can then spill out of you into the relationships with your coworkers. Maybe you have been operating under the assumption that to love someone you must appreciate all their actions.

Christ told us to love our enemies (Matthew 5:44). Just trying harder to get along with people or attempting to show love to them on our own produces a contrived love. *Agape* love is the real thing. When we love others with God-originated agape love, love that's passed on to us *through* Christ, we'll find ourselves actually being able to supernaturally love those we previously disdained or endured.

Attempting to drag people to God's love never works. "When it comes to the workplace, we are not called to bring people to Jesus but rather to bring Jesus to people."[1] This can be accomplished only in genuine love. Being a conduit for God's love to pour through us will cause people to realize that they're spiritually thirsty, and they'll come looking for the source of the powerful love we exude.

It's as God's love pours through us, uncontaminated by judgment, that people are drawn to God. Martin Luther is quoted as saying, "The curse of a godless man can sound more pleasant in God's ears than the Hallelujah of the pious."[2] You can successfully show acts of kindness to people, but if you have a heart that's judging them, the effect of the love will not last. Instead, our attempts will feel more like burrs that rub against their skin, causing irritation and sore spots. We may judge their lifestyle choices, colorful language, entertainment venues, or even their spiritual thirst, and in doing so we condemn and widen the chasm between us. Judgment is not our role. I find it fascinating that Jesus' interaction with the woman caught in adultery, as recorded in John 4, ends with Him telling her that He did not condemn her. The holy and sinless Son of God by virtue of His righteousness had every right to condemn, but He didn't. And neither should we. Condemnation deepens the chasm. Love and acceptance build bridges.

Enter into the Lives of Others

Corporate Chaplains is a ministry that is committed to taking Christ into the workplace. They're hired by the management of companies to come into the workplace to offer life coaching and spiritual friendship to the employees. The chaplain commits to pursuing three- to five-minute conversations with each employee per week. This usually starts by simply talking about the weather or the sports scores—everyday events to which everyone can relate.

Over the weeks this level of interaction progresses to asking what's happening in their lives. Bruce Mitchell, Canadian Director of Corporate Chaplains, has indicated that within three to six months of meeting employees his conversations with them have switched from the hockey scores to significant personal or family issues such as a son's addiction to cocaine, a daughter's unplanned pregnancy, or marital disagreements. When I heard Bruce tell of the opportunities Corporate Chaplains are presented with, it made me excited about how God could use us if we purposefully started to take a keen interest in the world of our coworkers.

Imagine the conversations that could develop if you asked the boss about her weekend. After her obligatory response that it was fine, you can take it one step further to show an increased interest in her by asking, "What did you do?" I realize that if you had never asked her about her weekend before this could be a huge step. Maybe you will need to take small steps, but each small step of genuine interest will soon lead to finding out more about her. She'll sense that you care, and human beings respond to care. The love that care and interest communicate becomes a magnet that's hard to resist.

If all it takes for people to feel cared for is five minutes once a week for five weeks, we've lost our argument that we don't have time. Certainly we have a fiduciary responsibility to not be spending our work hours on personal business, but meeting a colleague on the way to the restroom or a coffee break discussion could be a perfect opportunity to show interest in someone. We're not called to enter into the lifestyles of our coworkers, but we do need to enter into their lives.

Being present in people's lives will provide opportunities to love. What do I mean by *being present*? Presence begins with attentiveness to other people's situations. It's putting aside my agenda and entering their worlds solely for the purpose of understanding and loving them. Attentiveness also involves "setting some things aside" such as my interests and preoccupations. It also demands that I stop analyzing what I am hearing or rehearsing how I will respond; it also involves resisting the impulse to solve problems or fix things that appear broken."[3] It also means putting aside the desire to get a person saved. Simply being present communicates love.

Let Others Come into Your Life

Marilyn had worked in her government position for ten years. She was known as a strong leader, hard worker, dependable and caring of both staff and clients. She took an interest in the people around her, and employees clamored to be on her team. It was unusual for her to take a sick day, so when it was announced that she would be taking sick leave, the employees in the office were surprised and wondered what was going on.

Supposition trickled out that Marilyn had one ailment or another, but when the announcement was finally made that the multiple sclerosis she had battled for fifteen years had suddenly taken a turn for the worse and the prognosis was not good, everyone was dumbfounded. How had Marilyn hidden her health challenge so effectively? Why had she kept it a secret? People began to wonder if there were other things she had withheld from the team. As the office gossip spread, people began to share what they knew of Marilyn. It quickly became obvious that most people knew little about her other than the persona she had portrayed around the office. Who was this woman they had grown to appreciate at work?

Two months later, this same group of colleagues joined together to attend Marilyn's memorial service. As family and close friends stood up to eulogize her, these coworkers who had spent forty hours a week with Marilyn heard about a side of her they had no idea existed. Her trip to Asia had actually been to work in an orphanage. She volunteered on Wednesday evenings at a women's shelter. She taught Sunday School to four-year-olds every week. The type of woman described fit the character of the government employee they knew, but they had never been given a glimpse into the real Marilyn. Her coworkers were bewildered that she had never shared at the office about the faith that seemed so important to her outside of her job. Some left that service surmising that one's faith is to be kept private. Others concluded that Marilyn's faith and God had no true relevance to life. Still others felt confirmed in their approach to compartmentalizing their relationships with God.

Marilyn's story is tragic, because she missed a significant opportunity to live a fully integrated life that would have brought her faith to her workplace, impacted many people along the way, and broadened the effect of her legacy. Marilyn's choice to keep her personal life and faith private was rightly viewed by her coworkers as a lack of sharing herself, and in that lack of sharing they saw a withholding of love. She missed her chance to be an Esther who had been brought to that government office for such a time as this—to be a conduit of God's love to her coworkers.

If Marilyn had lived out the directive Christ gave to love others and to be involved in their lives, think about the added impact it could have had on her coworkers.

Here's another way to put it: You're here to be light, bringing out the God-colors in the world. God is not a secret to be kept. We're going public with this, as public as a city on a hill. If I make you light-bearers, you don't think I'm going to hide you under a bucket, do you? I'm putting you on a light stand. Now that I've put you there on a hilltop, on a light stand—shine! Keep open house; be generous with your lives. By opening up to others, you'll prompt people to open up with God, this generous Father in heaven (*Matthew 5:14-16, tm*).

Marilyn's unwillingness to let others into her life kept people from opening up to God. If we take Christ's words in Matthew 5 seriously, we can be assured that when we share what's going on in our lives, the Holy Spirit will use that to prompt hearts to open up to God. We're not responsible for getting people to respond to God. Our responsibility is to be authentic about what's going on in our lives, including what God is doing in our hearts.

Authenticity, Not Perfection

A pharisaical mindset would cause us to believe that we must have our lives impeccably together to portray a perfect example of God's love in order to draw anyone to Jesus. There are two fallacies in that way of thinking.

The first fallacy is that our best witness is a life that's perfect. I would argue that the opposite is true. Portraying perfection creates a relational chasm. Being authentic builds bridges. Our attempts to portray perfection have a negative effect on our ability to love people and to pass on God's love. People running around pretending to be perfect Christians are "actually doing grave damage. They are perpetuating the myth that Christians are better than anybody else and driving away those who truly need to receive God's love and forgiveness."[4] By our being authentic with people about our struggles and our failures, others will discover why we need God in our lives and will be willing to see that perhaps they, too, are in need of God's love and forgiveness.

In God's economy, everything is topsy-turvy. "Less is more. Lower is higher. Worse is better. Weaker is stronger. Showing our world our worst is going to do more for the gospel than showing the world our best."[5] I'm not suggesting we go out and flaunt or sensationalize our sin in hopes of strengthening our witness to others. Simply being real about who we are, what's going on in our lives, and the difference God's love has made to us will have a powerful effect on those with whom we share.

The second fallacy is that we draw people to Jesus. Wrong. God draws people to himself. "Long before he laid down earth's foundations, he had us in mind, had settled on us as the focus of his love, to be made whole and holy by his love. Long, long ago he decided to adopt us into his family through Jesus Christ. . . . He wanted us to enter into the celebration of his lavish gift-giving by the hand of his beloved Son" (Ephesians 1:3-6, TM).

Be Watchful

"My job is not to make something happen spiritually, but to discover what God is already doing and pour fuel on the fire."[6] Have you ever tried to start a fire in the rain or with wet wood? It's next to impossible. Our view of sharing our faith is that our coworkers are wet wood, because they have no interest in God or religion. Maybe it's true that they express no interest or they even convey an aversion to spiritual conversations. But rather than writing them off and looking for "drier wood," take a look with me at our core beliefs. What do we believe about the way each of us was created?

Scripture says that we're created in the image of God (Genesis 1:26), that the requirements of the law are written on our hearts (Romans 1:16), and that God has engraved eternity in the hearts of everyone (Ecclesiastes 3:11). God has stamped His reflection on our hearts, and since God is about love and relationship, that stamp acts as a continual pull to be in relationship with Him. Multitudes of people throughout history have spent their lives resisting that pull. Despite our resistance, the ramification of this holy stamp is that God the Creator is at work wooing each of us to himself.

This wooing may take the form of a beautiful sunrise, the birth of a child, the death of a loved one, or anything that seems to be bigger than we can fathom.

When we come into relationship with people at work and embrace the viewpoint that God is at work in all lives, this will move us from a wet wood-dry wood mentality to a belief that already there are live embers in their souls. This belief behooves the response to be watchful for opportunities where fuel can be added so the fire can grow.

How can we add fuel? Prayer is number one. If we try to reach out to people through our own human attempts, it will be as if we're spitting on the fire rather than adding fuel. "The prayer of a righteous man is powerful and effective" (James 5:16). As in everything else we do, we're completely dependent on the prompting of the Holy Spirit.

A number of years ago I read a wonderful novel called *The Heart Reader*.[7] It changed my perspective on the role of the Holy Spirit in my relationships. In this novel the character Sam receives the gift of being able to hear people's deepest heart cry. As he goes about his daily ritual of having breakfast at his local coffee shop, responding to the waitress's greeting, he realizes that he can hear the inner thoughts of her heart. He hears her think that a little rest could change her whole life.

At first he's bewildered that he's hearing much more than what her lips are conveying. Initially he resists, but he soon realizes that it's a *gift*. The premise of *The Heart Reader* is that all of us are given this gift by virtue of our connection to the Holy Spirit, who truly can read the heart of each of us. When we're attentive to the Holy Spirit, He'll give us a glimpse into the spiritual needs of others and then provide us the words to speak hope to them.

By being attentive to the Holy Spirit and getting to know our co-workers, God will reveal to you where there are live embers waiting for His fuel. We must be careful not to assume that pouring a can of gasoline is the best route. Sometimes just the gentle puff of an encouraging word or a sincere compliment enlivens the embers. Follow the prompting of the Holy Spirit, and you can be sure that the fuel will always be appropriate. If we try to do it under our own power, we can end up dowsing the fire or creating a flare-up that quickly flickers out. The emphasis must be on celebrating what God is doing in their lives, not judging what you think they're doing wrong.

Are you hoarding His love? Take the time and effort to love the people you work with. Be involved in their lives. Show genuine care to them. Be authentic about what's going on in your own life, and let people see that you're honest and forgive. The outcome will be an opportunity to talk with them about the love and hope that Jesus has given you. God's love is the one thing we can give away and yet never lose. That's a legacy worth leaving.

The Esther Connection

Arguments could be made that Esther hid her faith. Had she been more vocal about it earlier, Haman would never have gotten his plan past the king, and the subsequent massacre would never have happened. I don't pretend to understand God's way of doing things, but I do believe with all my heart that God put Esther where she needed to be at the time she needed to be there. Part of that plan involved her quietly living out her faith until such a time as He needed her to speak.

Mordecai, Esther's older and wiser mentor, understood the milieu of the palace. As an attendant in the king's court, he was part of the everyday happenings. Scripture does not give an explanation of Mordecai's reasoning for forbidding Esther to reveal her nationality or family background (Esther 2:10). We can only surmise that Mordecai must have seen reasons to keep this knowledge unrevealed.

From this side of history we can confirm that Mordecai had been led by God because He had a plan much greater than anyone could have imagined.

Had Esther been vocal about her heritage and faith upon entering the palace, things might have turned out very differently. But God had plans for Esther, "plans for good and not harm, plans to prosper and not harm, plans for hope and a future" (Jeremiah 29:11). Esther was able to speak of her faith at just the right time.

How did she know when the time was right? God's timing was not for her to speak at the first banquet. She relied on God's direction and revealed the thing most precious to her—her Jewish faith—at the second banquet. If only we were that attentive to God's leading—living out our faith and speaking at God's prompting! We can be assured that His timing will always be right and that the result will have eternal rewards.

Verses for Study

Romans 1:16-17
Matthew 28:16-20
Jeremiah 24:6-7
Ephesians 1:3-6
Ecclesiastes 3:11
Jeremiah 29:11
John 4:1-42
James 5:16
1 Peter 3:13-17

Questions for Reflection

1. In what ways have you been hesitant to let your coworkers gain a full perspective of who you are, including your faith in God?

2. What holds you back from getting involved or taking an interest in your coworkers' lives? What could you do differently?

3. Take the challenge to pray for opportunities to show love to your coworkers. Who do you have in your life that encourages you and holds you accountable to love your coworkers?

Epilogue

We took this journey knowing that the relational chasms within the workplace can be wide and numerous. Whether it's the boss whose weak leadership tempts us to usurp his or her authority, the slothful employee who threatens productivity, the dysfunctional team member who disengages, the chauvinistic male coworker who shreds our femininity, or the female colleague who agitates envy within us—we're given the task to build relational bridges to these and every person with whom we work. Each bridge is unique. Sin erodes. Love rebuilds. Godly legacies remain.

I trust that as you've read these pages you've picked up the challenge to love each person with whom you work. We're so limited on our own to do the building. But I can assure you with confidence that "There has never been the slightest doubt in my mind that the God who started this great work in you would keep at it and bring it to a flourishing finish on the very day Christ Jesus appears" (Philippians 1:6, TM).

If we've opened our hearts to God, "His divine power has given us everything we need for life and godliness through our knowledge of him who called us by his own glory and goodness" (2 Peter 1:3). We have at our disposal every relational tool we'll ever need.

Ladies, each of you is a modern-day Esther. God has placed you in your current workplace for a very specific purpose. I beseech you to go to work each day with an open heart and with eyes and ears attuned to the purpose God has for you. Live each day and enter each relationship with the conviction that you're at this place "for such a time as this."

Notes

Chapter 1

1. Patrick Lencioni, *The Five Dysfunctions of a Team* (San Francisco: Jossey-Bass, 2002), 195.

2. Ibid., 196.

3. Ibid., 197.

Chapter 2

1. C. S. Lewis, *Mere Christianity*, as quoted in Wayne Martindale and Jerry Root, *The Quotable Lewis* (Wheaton, Ill.: Tyndale House Publishers, 1989), 318.

Chapter 3

1. Robert Feldman, *The Liar in Your Life* (New York: Hachette Book Group, 2009), 14-15.

2. Dallas Willard, *The Spirit of the Disciplines* (San Francisco: Harper and Row, 1988), 165.

3. David G. Benner, *Sacred Companions* (Downers Grove, Ill.: InterVarsity Press, 2002), 51.

4. Henry Cloud, *Integrity* (New York: Harper and Row, 2006), 31.

5. Stephen R. Covey, *Seven Habits of Highly Effective People.*

6. John MacArthur, *The MacArthur Bible Commentary* (Nashville: Thomas Nelson Publishers, 2005), 555.

Chapter 4

1. Alister McGrath, *The NIV Thematic Reference Bible* (Grand Rapids: Zondervan Publishing House, 1999), 5790.

2. Mary Ellen Ashcroft, *The Temptations Women Face* (Downers Grove, Ill.: InterVarsity Press, 1991), 104.

3. Dallas Willard, *Renovation of the Heart* (Colorado Springs: NavPress, 2002), 138.

4. Greta Sheppard, *Excuse Me, Your Unforgiveness Is Showing* (Sheppard Ministries, 2003), 26.

5. This idea was gleaned from a conversation with Greta Sheppard, author of *Excuse Me, Your Unforgiveness Is Showing*, Oct. 9, 2009.

6. MacArthur, *The MacArthur Bible*, 1158.

7. Hayle DiMarco, *Mean Girls All Grown Up* (Grand Rapids: Fleming H. Revell, 2005), 91.

Chapter 5

1. "Adam's legacy of relating" and "Christ's legacy of relating" were terms used by Larry Crabb at his Advanced School of Spiritual Directing in Colorado Springs, July 2006.

2. Teresa of Avila, *Interior Castle* (Garden City, N.Y.: Doubleday, 1961), 10.

3. <www.parstimes.com/women/women_ancient_persia.html>.

Chapter 6

1. Ruth Myers, *Christ Life* (Sisters, Oreg.: Multnomah Publishers, 2005), 130-31.

Chapter 7

1. Lencioni, *The Five Dysfunctions of a Team*, vii.

2. I want to give credit for much of the material in this chapter to my mentor, Florence Littauer, who has taught the "Personalities" for more than thirty years. For further information, go to <www.classervices.com> or one of the many books written by Florence Littauer and Marita Littauer on the topic of personalities.

3. Tom Rath, *Strengths Finder 2.0* (New York: Gallup Press, 2007), iv.

4. Florence Littauer and Marita Littauer, *Succeeding at Work by Solving the Personality Puzzle* (Grand Rapids: Fleming H. Revell, 1992), 15.

Chapter 8

1. Robert Frost, <www.famousquotesandauthors.com>, December 15, 2009.

2. Jim Collins, *Good to Great* (New York: Harper Collins, 2001), 20.

3. Ibid., 27.

4. Ibid., 35.

5. Ibid.

6. Steve R. Covey, *Principle-Centered Leadership* (New York: Fireside Books, 1992) 248-49.

7. Ibid.

8. Lisa Haneberg, "Management Craft," <www.managementcraft.com/2008/12/why-managers-is-like-a-gps.html>, December 7, 2008. (Web site no longer available)

9. Larry Crabb, *Connecting* (Nashville: Word Publishing, 1997), 53.

10. Michael M. Lombardo and Robert W. Eichinger, *FYI: For Your Improvement* (Minneapolis: Lominger Limited, 2000), 38.

11. Max Lucado, *Facing Your Giants* (Nashville: Word Publishing, 2006), 133-34.

Chapter 9

1. Mike Bonem and Roger Patterson, *Leading from the Second Chair* (San Francisco: Jossey-Bass, 2005), 45.

2. Ibid., 133.

3. Lombardo and Eichinger, *For Your Improvement*, 20.

Chapter 10

1. <www.news.bbc.co.uk>, September 3, 2009.

2. <www.dol.gov/wb/stats/main.htm>, September 3, 2009.

3. <www.thestar.com/news/gta/article/691396>, September 8, 2009.

4. "Think It Over," *Quiet Moments in the Presence of God* (Bloomington, Minn.: Bethany House, 2005), 172.

5. Nancy Beach, *Gifted to Lead* (Grand Rapids: Zondervan Publishing House, 2008).

6. Jane Stephens and Stephen Zades, *Mad Dogs, Dreamers, and Sages: Growth in the Age of Ideas* (New York: Elouda Press, 2003), 92.

7. Shannon Ethridge, *Every Woman's Battle* (Colorado Springs: WaterBrook Press, 2003), 67.

Chapter 11

1. DiMarco, *Mean Girls All Grown Up*, 22.

2. Ibid., 22-23.

3. Joseph M. Stowell, *The Weight of Your Words* (Chicago: Moody Press, 1998), 48.

4. Ibid., 52.

5. DiMarco, *Mean Girls All Grown Up,* 162.

Chapter 12

1. William Carr Peel and Walt Larimore, *Going Public with Your Faith* (Grand Rapids: Zondervan Publishing House, 2003), 77.

2. Martin Luther, as quoted in Dietrich Bonhoeffer, *Life Together* (San Francisco: Harper and Row Publishers, 1954), 9.

3. Benner, *Sacred Companions*, 50.

4. John Fischer, *12 Steps for the Recovering Pharisee (like me)* (Minneapolis: Bethany House Publishers, 2000), 160.

5. Ibid., 161.

6. William Carr Peel, Walt Larimore, <www.24sevenfaith.com>, March 26, 2009.

7. Terri Blackstock, *The Heart Reader* (Nashville: Word Publishing, 2000).

"This engaging book challenges women to take a journey of self-discovery in all relationships. It effectively integrates spirituality and psychology to take women to the soul of their frustrations in life."

—WENDY LOWE,
executive director, Calgary Pregnancy Care Centre

Bridge the gap to better connections.

Through encouragement and introspection, this practical book helps you connect your spiritual life and your daily interactions with the people you love as God begins to change you from the inside out.

A Woman and Her Relationships
Transforming the Way We Connect
ISBN: 978-0-8341-2338-0

www.BeaconHillPress.com
1.800.877.0700